Alison Lurie

Twayne's United States Authors Series

Frank Day, Editor
Clemson University

TUSAS 602

ALISON LURIE
©Jimm Roberts/Orlando 1989

Alison Lurie

Richard Hauer Costa

Texas A&M University

Twayne Publishers / New York

Maxwell Macmillan Canada / Toronto

Maxwell Macmillan International / New York Oxford Singapore Sydney

Alison Lurie
Richard Hauer Costa

Copyright 1992 by Twayne Publishers

Twayne Publishers
Macmillan Publishing Company
866 Third Avenue
New York, New York 10022

Maxwell Macmillan Canada, Inc.
1200 Eglinton Avenue East
Suite 200
Don Mills, Ontario M3C 3N1

Macmillan Publishing Company is part of the Maxwell Communication
Group of Companies.

Library of Congress Cataloging-in-Publication Data

Costa, Richard Hauer.
    Alison Lurie / Richard Hauer Costa.
        p. cm. – (Twayne's United States authors series; TUSAS 602)
    Includes bibliographical references and index.
    ISBN 0-8057-7634-6
    1. Lurie, Alison – Criticism and interpretation. I. Title. II. Series.
PS3562.U7Z63   1992
813'.54 – dc20   91-45881
                                      CIP

For Pamela Lynn Palmer

who like this book's subject is a feminist,
but never doctrinaire, and on whose critiques I have relied

Contents

Preface

Today it is not possible to *discover* a new book the way one could 40 years ago. To do so requires freedom from the influence of Manhattan publicity campaigns intent on making even the most mediocre books best sellers. And it requires ignorance of an author's previous literary efforts and reputation. Nonetheless, I came close to managing such a discovery of Alison Lurie's *Foreign Affairs.* I had read none of her earlier works and had heard a great deal about only one of them, *The War between the Tates.* Consequently, *Foreign Affairs* took me entirely by surprise.

Who can say what it is about a book that hooks you from the first word, leading you to speed through it in only two or three sittings? *Foreign Affairs* begins as follows: "On a cold blowy February day a woman is boarding the 10 A.M. flight to London, followed by an invisible dog. The woman's name is Virginia Miner: she is fifty-four years old, small, plain, and unmarried – the sort of character no one notices, though she is an Ivy League college professor who has published several books and has a well-established reputation in the expanding field of children's literature." Lurie's ability to make an unprepossessing person noteworthy, her promise of a Henry Jamesian plot in the American abroad, and the immediacy of her prose style engaged me right away.

After *Foreign Affairs,* I read the balance of her work, which to date includes eight novels, two nonfiction books, and several collections of children's stories. Her fiction demonstrates a progressive refining of craft and deepening of themes. Up to and including *Foreign Affairs,* Lurie's novels are thematically cumulative. They record the progress of the protagonist from innocence to awareness, typically featuring a heroine who has reached a cross-roads in marriage, usually to an academic. Lack of personal and professional fulfillment ultimately pushes the heroine outside the marriage, often to a passionate, giving lover, wherein the experience of sexual liberation leads to at least a partial liberation and discovery of self. In the case of *Foreign Affairs,* the protagonist, Virginia Miner, is unmarried.

Like the women in Lurie's other books, however, she is emotionally transformed as the result of an affair. Time, I believe, will bear out my belief that *The Truth about Lorin Jones*, at this writing Lurie's most recent novel, marks a crucial transition from books about the wives, husbands, and children of academe into broader fictional territory.

Lurie's predilection for children and their literature informs much of her fiction. Among her novels this interest is most obvious in *Only Children*, a story quite sympathetic to the plight of two eight-year-old girls as they try to make sense of the world. Lurie's interest in children's literature is of course also expressed in the three volumes of stories she collected expressly for children. Lurie's retelling of classic fairy tales in the 1980 volume, *Clever Gretchen and Other Forgotten Folktales*, extracts folktales from a rich literature – stories that project women as courageous and enterprising, able to bring down giants and outwit Satan rather than passively await Prince Charming. Two other volumes for children, *Fabulous Beasts* (1981) and *The Heavenly Zoo* (1980), are aimed at freeing young imaginations; the first brings together stories of legendary wildlife (for example, "The Basilisk" and "The Vegetable Lambs"), and the second recounts the stories of the stars as culled from Greek, biblical, Indonesian, and American Indian sources. Discussion of these books lies outside the scope of this volume, which is devoted to Lurie's major writings for adults.

Alison Lurie opens with a partly biographical chapter. I then devote chapter 2 to a brief background of the once-stable institution of marriage as fiction's main event and chapters 3 and 4 to the collapse of marriage in Alison Lurie's novels through *The War between the Tates*. Lurie's career as a novelist began in the early 1960s, when the women's movement, fired by such works as Betty Friedan's *Feminine Mystique*, revolutionized our view of men's and women's roles and our concept of the nuclear family. The era could well be known by one of Lurie's favorite words, "the *subversive* sixties."

In chapter 5, I link Lurie's collected writings on the subversive in children's literature, titled *Don't Tell the Grown-ups*, with *Only Children*, in which the subversive impulses of adults are exposed by two eight-year-old girls. I move to *Foreign Affairs* in chapter 6, and in chapter 7 discuss *The Language of Clothes*. This nonfiction work has been praised for its shrewd insights into how fashion reflects changing sex roles, political upheavals, and class structure. It also illuminates Lurie's own use of dress in her novels as a device for fictive discovery.

Chapter 8 is devoted to an anomaly in Lurie's writings, a novel that has many elements of science fiction–*Imaginary Friends*. In chapter 9 I assess Lurie's standing with a wide spectrum of critics–reviewers in the popular press as well as academics–while chapter 10 focuses on *The Truth about Lorin Jones*, a book that I believe presages new directions for her. Finally, the appendix traces the evolution of the character Leonard Zimmern, who appears in a number of Lurie's novels.

I am grateful to the critics and reviewers who increasingly accord Alison Lurie consideration as a novelist of stature. I want especially to note my debt to one of them, Katharine M. Rogers, for her essay "Alison Lurie: The Uses of Adultery."

I wish to thank Alison Lurie for taking time from her fall 1989 classes at Cornell University to discuss her life and writings with me and also for her permission to quote from her published writings.

Pamela Lynn Palmer, a poet and biographer, read most of the chapters as they were written and offered valuable suggestions. I thank her not only for her advice but for her moral support from the beginning.

Janis Stout, my colleague and a devoted Lurie reader, also read much of the manuscript. If I have not acted substantively on her criticisms, the fault is wholly mine.

J. F. Hopkins, a novelist and a close friend for a half-century, has for most of those years directed me to materials I would otherwise have missed, and never more so than during the work on this book.

Frank Tuohy, the British novelist and short story writer, told me of the high esteem in which Alison Lurie is held in England. He alerted me to Lurie's kinships with Barbara Pym, Anthony Powell, and Evelyn Waugh in the reintroduction of characters from book to book.

I am grateful to Dorothy Van Riper, my colleague and a longtime devotee of Alison Lurie. Her general encouragement in one of my many areas of ignorance–children's literature–helped.

By an accident of informal conversation, I found in my friend, Jack K. Campbell of the College of Education at Texas A&M, a source of information that helped me better understand Alison Lurie's writings on subversive children's books.

Elena B. Fimmano of Utica, New York, made her exhaustive notes on *Foreign Affairs* available to me.

Special thanks to Frank Day, my field editor, and to India Koopman at Twayne for their readings, the most exhaustive and acute of my experience. Liz Traynor Fowler merits my appreciation for her caring solicitude during this book's long gestation.

Finally, first, last, and always, my gratitude beyond words to Jo, my wife of 40 years, for sparing me in unnumbered ways.

Chronology

1926	Alison Lurie born 3 September in Chicago, the older of two daughters, to Harry and Bernice (Stewart) Lurie.
1930	Family moves to New York City and then to White Plains, Westchester County.
1943	Lurie graduates from Cherry Lawn School, Darien, Connecticut.
1946	Wins New Direction poetry contest; stories published in *The Woman's Press* and *Commentary;* graduates from Radcliffe College, A.B., magna cum laude (January); "Three Poems" published in *Poetry* (June).
1947	Editorial assistant, Oxford University Press, New York City.
1948	Marries Jonathan Peale Bishop, a graduate student in English at Harvard University, 10 September.
1953	Birth of first son, John.
1954	Moves with husband to Amherst College, Amherst, Massachusetts, where he teaches English.
1955	Birth of second son, Jeremy.
1956	Unexpected death of close friend, poet V. R. (Bunny) Lang, 29 July.
1957	Moves with husband to Los Angeles, where he teaches English at the University of California.
1959	*V. R. Lang: A Memoir* published privately.
1960	Birth of third son, Joshua.
1961	Moves with husband to Cornell University, where he teaches English.

1962	First novel, *Love and Friendship*.
1963-1964	Yaddo Foundation Fellowships, Saratoga Springs, New York.
1965	*The Nowhere City;* Guggenheim Fellowship.
1966	Yaddo Foundation Fellowship.
1967	*Imaginary Friends;* Rockefeller Foundation grant.
1969	*Real People;* begins teaching career at Cornell University.
1973	Promoted to associate professor.
1974	*The War between the Tates*.
1975	Separates from husband; *V. R. Lang: A Memoir* published as introduction to Lang's *Poems & Plays*.
1976	Promoted to professor.
1977	*The War between the Tates* produced as television movie.
1978	American Academy of Arts and Letters award in literature.
1979	*Only Children*.
1980	*The Heavenly Zoo: Legends and Tales of the Stars; Clever Gretchen and Other Forgotten Folk Tales* (both juvenile).
1981	*Fabulous Beasts* (juvenile); *The Language of Clothes*.
1984	*Foreign Affairs;* American Book Award nomination in fiction for *Foreign Affairs*.
1985	Pulitzer Prize in fiction for *Foreign Affairs*. Divorced from husband.
1988	*The Truth about Lorin Jones*.
1990	*Don't Tell the Grown-ups: Subversive Children's Literature*.

Chapter One

"Chastening Morals with Ridicule"

Life of the Mind

Alison Lurie was reared in a family in which ideas, especially sociopolitical ideas, were daily currency. She was born in Chicago on 3 September 1926, the oldest of two daughters of Harry and Bernice (Stewart) Lurie. Her Latvian-born father was a scholar and a teacher of social work with a graduate degree from the University of Michigan. He later became the founder and executive director of the Council of Jewish Federations and Welfare Funds. He and his wife, a former journalist with the Detroit *Free Press*, were Socialists. Alison recalls Norman Thomas, the perennial socialist presidential candidate, visiting her parents at home.

The Lurie family moved to New York City when Alison was four years old and soon afterward to what was then a rural suburb of White Plains in Westchester County. She grew up with her sister, Jennifer, and attended private schools and, briefly, the public high school before enrolling in a progressive preparatory school, Cherry Lawn in Darien, Connecticut.

She was, by her own estimate, "a skinny, plain, odd-looking little girl." A birth injury caused "atrophy of the facial muscles that pulled my mouth sideways whenever I opened it to speak and turned my smile into a sort of sneer."[1] Without a trace of self-consciousness, she told me that there was often some damage during high-forceps deliveries. The alternative, then as now, was a Caesarian – far more dangerous in 1926, when Lurie was born, because there were no antibiotics. The damage in her case included an injured left ear and loss of hearing on that side.

In a memoir she wrote at 55, Lurie recalls being considered "too clever for her own good" but deficient in charm and regard for others. Skills that other 10-year-olds took for granted – riding a bike, singing, playing games – were denied her. She believed that "nobody would wish to marry me and I would never have any of the children whose names and sexes I had chosen at an earlier time and more ignorant age. I would be an ugly old maid, the card in the pack that everyone tried to get rid of" ("No One Asked," 13).

Inventing stories, drawing, baking brownies, and making rag rugs saved her childhood. If Alison Lurie was not to be told she was "perfectly lovely," she would settle for next best: perfection of the work.

> With a pencil and paper I could revise the world. I could move mountains; I could fly over Westchester at night in a winged clothes basket; I could call up a brown-and-white-spotted milkgiving dragon to eat the neighbor who had told me and my sister not to walk through her field and bother her cows. And a little later, when I tried nonfiction, I found that without actually lying I could describe events and persons in such a way that my readers would think of them as I chose. ("No One Asked," 13)

Forty years later she would reinvoke her early years by unleashing two girls, Mary Ann and Lolly, to deflate adult posturing in *Only Children* (1979).

Writing was a kind of "witch's spell" that held her in thrall through her years at Radcliffe. As a senior she won a New Directions poetry contest, which resulted in the appearance of three poems in *Poetry*. During the 1946-47 academic year her stories appeared in *Commentary* and *Woman's Press*. Lurie discounted these early efforts as "clumsy apprentice spells." After graduation Lurie moved to New York City and by the winter of 1947 was working as an editorial assistant at Oxford University Press. The habit of writing continued, but little saw print. Her friends, seeing how many rejection slips she received, encouraged her to spend less time writing. By the age of 28 she had had no acceptance in eight years. When her second novel was turned down by six publishers, she stopped writing altogether.

Having escaped her fear of becoming an "ugly old maid," Lurie had by this time married Jonathan Peale Bishop, son of the poet John Peale Bishop. The couple moved to western Massachusetts, where Bishop was an instructor at Amherst College. Lurie had also become a mother. She would long remember her husband's words during those days: "After all, Alison, nobody is asking you to write a novel" ("No One Asked," 13).

This was the 1950s, "when having a family was supposed to make a woman perfectly contented unless she was very immature, selfish or neurotic," Lurie recalls. "I told myself that my life was rich and full. Everybody else seemed to think so. Only I knew that, right at the center, it was false and empty. I wasn't what I was pretending to be. I didn't like staying home and taking care of little children; I was restless, impatient, ambitious" ("No One Asked," 47).

What delivered Lurie was her first experience of the death of a close friend. V. R. (Bunny) Lang, who died of Hodgkins disease in 1956, was a founder of the Poets' Theatre and a gifted poet, playwright, and actress "whose eccentric vitality had made existence more interesting and more difficult for everyone she knew" ("No One Asked," 47). Disturbed by how quickly even someone like Bunny Lang could be forgotten, Lurie determined to write down everything she could recall to save the memory of her friend from oblivion. From the memoirist, the novelist emerged.

Novelist as Memoirist

Only a writer with the instincts of a fictionist could have written a memoir so novelistically true. "It gives the reader what one would have thought only Bunny herself, alive, could have provided, that is, a projection of the spirit from which her work sprang."[2] So wrote Lang's husband, Bradley Phillips.

Writing the memoir was a life-changing event. This was Lurie's first experience of the death of anyone her own age. She has never forgotten that Hodgkin's disease became treatable in the early 1960s, soon after the death of her friend. Working on the memoir also had the effect of taking Lurie away from the conventional duties of wife and mother. In describing the search for creative fulfillment of an engaging eccentric who was also – and perhaps necessarily – a narcissist, Lurie had to deal with the defenses erected by a sufferer from certain personality disorders who is also highly talented. For the first time Lurie witnessed the ways entrenched academics stifle innovation. And, more important to later themes in her work, she placed under a humane spotlight the life of a determined and able original whose megalomania frustrated her own designs at every turn. Lurie's compassion for her subject precludes condescension or pity. What comes across to the reader is her sense of the sheer difficulty of living.

Lurie's true genre was to be the novel of manners. Her province would be those special attitudes, gestures, and responses of persons in harmony – or more often in disharmony – with a certain class at a certain time. She had located it early in the novels of Jane Austen and had written her senior paper at Radcliffe on the heightened comedy of the Jacobean Age. In her portrayal of Bunny Lang Lurie had found her impelling fictive cause: the way tensions within a class or between classes make comedy and the innumerable ways that style and personality shape each other.

We are introduced to Bunny Lang as a builder of appearances. From her theatrical ventures, costumes became means to accommodate the regular variance in her weight from 125 to 150 pounds. Nothing about her remained a single indelible image. There was something childlike and malleable in her face, not only in the full pout but in the sense of being molded in clay. She was an actress both in and out of the theater. But she was also very much the playwright, making up roles for her friends rather than seeing them for themselves.

> Bunny did treat everyone, however unimportant, as a person – as a person, but not as themselves. Instead of bothering to unearth their half-formed individuality, she spontaneously invented an interesting character for whomever she met, linking them, for the moment, with her. . . . Thus it might be said that . . . the character of everyone who knew Bunny is partly her creation. (*Lang*, 27-28)

Once she knew she was mortally ill, Bunny "played at dying as if she would make death just one more costume," writes Lurie.

> Sometimes she would behave as if she had never heard of doctors or their advice, up all night dancing and all day at the beach, and then anyone who sympathized with her or tried to make things easier for her (helping her out of a car or down steps, for instance) was fixed with a withering look. At other

times she played the part of a desperate invalid so dramatically that any solici-
tous act or speech took on the air of a bunch of violets dropped on a great
battlefield. *(Lang,* 51)

The appeal of so skilled a puppeteer of personality to a novelist
in the making cannot be overstated. Lurie's remembrance of her
friend surely taught her that manners, when marshalled to defend
against vulnerability, actually court disaster. Lurie's major novels are
about such disasters.

Breakthroughs

The year that Bunny Lang died, 1965, was also the year Lurie
reached 30, and it marked a turning point in her life. If writing the
memoir freed her imagination, moving to Los Angeles with her family
in 1957, when her husband accepted a teaching job at the University
of California, freed her from the small-town domesticity of Amherst.
The Nowhere City, published in 1956, conveys the culture shock of
Katherine Cattleman, whose New England upbringing clashes with
the manners and mores of Los Angeles. But Lurie was to write a
novel about Amherst first. In Jane Austen fashion, she titled it *Love
and Friendship* (1962).

The book was published on the recommendation of a friend's
brother, the writer Max Wilk, who knew an editor at Macmillan. In
retrospect, it is perhaps too easy to see *Love and Friendship* as a
"rehearsal" for *The War between the Tates,* appearing 12 years later.
Both are about infidelity, and both satirize academic life. "Of
course," Lurie comments, "I couldn't 'rehearse' for something I
could have no idea was coming up."[3]

What is undeniable is that "Lurie Country" is often an isolated
college town, in which there lives a family – a professor, his wife, and
their children – whose emotional lives Lurie scrutinizes. "I have to
write about things I know," she told an interviewer in 1986, "and I
happen to know what family life is about."[4] Lurie, now divorced,
also knows what the dismantling of marriage and family is about.
Marital tension looms in her work. Her protagonists are usually
women, and her women generally are, like herself, well-educated,
sophisticated members of the upper-middle class. Their dissatisfactions, she believes, stem from "an anomaly of history." Women of

her age and social class were at a disadvantage in raising their families. "Our mothers often had help bringing up their children and running the household. They had time to go to museums, see plays and films, have a life of the mind. My generation happens to be the one that has had to carry domestic duties almost wholly on our own shoulders. Coming out of good schools that, in a sense, prepared us for lives like those our mothers had, we felt we had been let down" (Conversation).

Awareness of unfulfilled lives did not begin with the 1960s. "Some of our mothers were unhappy – no question about it – but there was just no alternative. When women of my generation and after feel oppressed, we can do something about it" (Conversation). Many of Lurie's heroines hazard choices that have traditionally been anathema to marriage. Because adultery is no longer so shameful or stigmatizing, she does not hesitate to deploy it for both satiric effect and intellectual exploration of character.

Her heroines, for all – or perhaps because of – their inherent good taste and self-control, are "especially susceptible to the Call of the Wild and the perfectly rational processes of self deception," as Sara Sanborn observes. "Their carefully constructed lives and self-images . . . break up on the rocks of the irrational, to which they have been lured by the siren song of sheer sexual energy."[5] This strong summons to pleasure is balanced by the urge to live decently and with candor. Lurie's women, then, play a variation on the story of innocence meeting experience. It is here that Alison Lurie locates her fictional *metier.*

Foreign Affairs, which takes place in London and includes as characters a coterie of socialites as well as American academics, signifies a departure from Lurie's traditional locale and subject matter. Her most recent novel, *The Truth about Lorin Jones,* which closes in Key West and depicts the search of an unsuccessful painter for the truth about the life of another artist, now dead, represents an even greater breakthrough for Lurie in terms of subject, as will be discussed in the last chapter of this volume. Nonetheless, both novels are in keeping with Lurie's maxim of writing about what she knows and reflect changes in her own life. Lurie, who has taught part-time at Cornell University for 21 years, has for the past 10 years done most of her writing in her second home in Key West. Lurie also makes an annual trip to London.

Like all of her novels, however, *Foreign Affairs* and *The Truth about Lorin Jones* are evidence of the author's satirical sensibility. Lurie is quick to expose the disguises men and women adopt to hide from one another and from themselves. Present in all of her work is her intent, like Bernard Shaw's, to "chasten morals with ridicule."

Chapter Two

Marriage as Fiction's Main Event

Adultery as Transforming

The novels of Alison Lurie take the question posed by singer Peggy Lee in the ballad "Is That All There Is?"; apply it to marriage; and answer – resolutely but without zest – No. From the opening sentence of her *Love and Friendship* ("The day on which Emily Stockwell Turner fell out of love with her husband began much like other days.") to Erica Tate's sense, five novels later, that the rules for domestic tranquility are changing too fast and that she has been "shot forward into the wrong time,"[1] Lurie has charted the heartbeat of the institution and found the pulsations irregular. Full recovery is unlikely; accommodation may be possible at best.

Marriage had also long been the central subject for what Tony Tanner calls the "bourgeois novel."[2] Traditionally, he writes, marriage has been a means by which society attempts to bring into harmonious alignment patterns of passions and patterns of property. . . . For bourgeois society marriage is the all-subsuming, all-organizing, all-containing contract. . . . The bourgeois novelist has no choice but to engage the subject of marriage in one way or another, at no matter what extreme of celebration or contestation." Tanner argues persuasively that the change in the "essentiality" of bourgeois marriage – its loss of absoluteness – signaled a change in the relationship between novelist and reader. "We may say that as the contract between man and wife loses its sense of necessity and binding power, so does the contract between novelist and reader. . . . In confronting the problems of marriage and adultery, the bourgeois novel finally has to confront not only the provisionality of social laws and rules and structures but the provisionality of its own procedures and assumptions" (Tanner, 15).

9

Lurie sounds the deathknell of marriage almost from the first page of *The War between the Tates*. "In the abstract," Erica Tate "hated Hitler, Joseph McCarthy, Lee Harvey Oswald, etc. but never anyone she had to live with and should have loved–had for years and years and years warmly loved." What had happened? The children she loved, "her dear Muffy and Jeffo," had become buried "somewhere inside the monstrous lodgers who had taken over their minds and bodies" (*The Tates*, 6-7). They were now alien to her. Her husband, Brian, an Ivy League academic, had been unfaithful, and she detested him for this betrayal. *The War between the Tates* is one of contemporary fiction's major frontal assaults on marriage as a given, both of traditional society and of traditional fiction. No novel depicting middle-class family life in the 1960s shows more powerfully the impact of adultery on marriage. As will be shown in the next two chapters, Lurie's adultery plots allow her to explore the potentialities of her unfulfilled wives. By breaking out of marriage, they confront new truths.

Of course, adultery has long appeared in the novel and occurred in Elizabethan and Restoration plays before the novel became a recognized genre. But it rarely, if ever, jeopardized the institution of marriage. (It is only William Wycherley's deft manipulation of Horner's promiscuous cuckolding that allows the forthright Margery in *The Country Wife* (1675) to turn him away, remain with her "musty husband," and acquiesce in politeness. Intermarital gamesplay in Restoration comedy never threatens the sanctity of the institution.)

"What therefore God hath joined together, let not man put asunder" (Matthew 19:6). So goes the biblical injunction often invoked at Christian weddings. It is only when marriage is viewed as the invention of man and is felt to be the central contract on which all others in some way depend that adultery becomes not an incidental deviance from the social structure but an attack on it.

The modern response to marital problems is often divorce. Yet both Tanner and Lurie eschew it. "In none of the novels I wish to consider does divorce occur," Tanner writes, "nor is it felt to offer any *radical* solutions to the problems that have arisen. It is as if the novelist realized that divorce was a piece of surface temporizing, a forensic palliative to cloak and muffle the profoundly disjunctive reverberations and implications of adultery" (Tanner, 17-18). Whether or not Lurie falls within Tanner's conjectural terrain is impossible to ascertain. Still, divorce is never a fait accompli in any of her novels.

Marriage and the Novel: A Brief Exploration from *Pamela* to *The War between the Tates*

"The most important mediation procedure that attempts to harmonize the natural, the familial, the social, and even the transcendental is, of course, marriage" (Tanner, 16). The reality of marriage, of course, has often fallen short of this traditional ideal, with varying implications for women. It is women, as Tanner writes, who have most often been vulnerable to its gyrations. So too in the novel, the meaning of marriage in a woman's life and the expectations about her behavior in the marriage are very different from a man's, and far more circumscribed.

Jane Miller, who in *Women Writing about Men* (1986) studies the novels of eight women, beginning with Jane Austen and concluding with Alice Walker, accepts the importance of marriage in fiction. But she clearly delineates its role in the lives of female characters as opposed to male. As "long as the ending, the completion, of a woman's story is marriage to a man, a woman's adventure will not be a man's adventure. Its time scale will be different, for a woman's adventure will occupy only a small strip of her life, when she is very young. It will test her and put her through her paces; but the proceedings, like the outcome, will be circumscribed by the conventions of the society she inhabits, which will figure in her adventure as protagonists bent above all on controlling what she can tell and how."[3] Miller goes on to suggest that most women's novels seek to extricate not only their heroines but their authors from charges of "abnormality." If marriage is the "normal" ending to a woman's adventure and the necessary completion of a woman's existence, occurrences that divert a woman from that outcome may be read as frivolous (as in Restoration comedy), unfortunate (as in early novels like *Pamela* and *Moll Flanders*), even perverse (as with Sue Bridehead in Hardy's *Jude the Obscure*).

If the English novel began with *Pamela* (1740), the notion that a woman's life is defined by her marriageability was deeply entrenched from the beginning. In Samuel Richardson's landmark book, the

astute farmer's daughter, Pamela, must exercise a cunning that is at
least equal to that of her pursuer, Mr. B., to beguile him into
marriage. To the modern reader, *Pamela* is not a moral fable but a
comedy of manners in which the author has combined innocence
and cunning in a protagonist who needs just the right amount of
both to break through the tightly locked eighteenth-century caste
system. Robert A. Donovan sees as standard equipment Pamela's
"dual safety device," which always keeps her virtue intact: her own
propensity to throw a fit when hard pressed and Mr. B.'s shame and
ineptitude at the prospect of stooping to rape. Donovan locates the
suspense of the novel in the recurring need for Pamela to improvise
in a difficult social game "whose rules she is ignorant of."[4] He
demonstrates effectively how Pamela turns her principal disabil-
ity–her inferior status–into an impregnable fortress. The larger
game she is playing–the winning of Mr. B.'s hand in marriage–provides in *Pamela* perhaps the earliest manual of the ground
rules for attaining marriage, the era's only buffer against spinster-
hood and prostitution.

Forty years later, Frances Burney's title character in *Evelina*
writes to Mr. Villars on her marriage day, "All is over . . . and the fate
of your Evelina is decided!"[5] Katharine M. Rogers, in her essential
essay on "The Uses of Adultery" in Alison Lurie, observes that
Evelina's joyous fatalism records the assumption, dominant in both
traditional fiction and society for over 200 years, that a woman's
social role should be fulfilled in marriage.

Jane Austen, whose thematic territory is closer to Lurie's than
any writer of the previous century except Henry James, applies to
tensions between the sexes the refinements of irony. Nowhere, of
course, is her technique illustrated better than in the opening
sentence of *Pride and Prejudice:* "It is a truth universally acknowl-
edged that a single man in possession of a good fortune must be in
want of a wife." She thus alludes to the courtship of the proud Mr.
Darcy, who aims to adhere to a code of conduct determined largely
by class distinctions, and Elizabeth Bennet, who aspires to a code
where humane impulses are not frustrated by class.

In *Pride and Prejudice* (1813), Austen conducts the courtship
with all the delicacy of the minuet, whose patterned responses in the
openings and closings between partners camouflage a power struggle between two admirable persons that only marriage can tran-

scend. But what if the marriage falls short? In their novelistic studies of bad marriages, *Middlemarch* (1872) and *Portrait of a Lady* (1881), George Eliot and Henry James create wives who a century later, in Erica Tate's "wrong time," would have acted differently.

Eliot's heroine, Dorothea Brooke, honeymooning in Rome with Casaubon, her pedantic middle-aged husband, "is discovered in a fit of weeping six weeks after her wedding." If called upon to explain herself, Eliot writes, Dorothea

> could only have done so in some such general words as I have already used: to have been driven to be more particular would have been like trying to give a history of the lights and shadows; for that new real future which was replacing the imaginary drew its material from the endless minutiae by which her view of Mr. Casaubon and her wifely relation, now that she was married to him, was gradually changing with the secret motion of a watch-hand from what it had been in her maiden dream.[6]

Eliot spares Dorothea Brooke a devastatingly sterile married life such as that with which Alison Lurie confronts Erica Tate 130 years later. Mercifully for Dorothea and the institution of marriage, Casaubon soon dies, freeing Dorothea to pursue her maidenly ideal of marriage.

In James's *Portrait of a Lady*, Isabel Archer is permitted to confront her sexuality more directly than any Jamesian woman. Yet, even with an ideal companion in the wings, Isabel vows to continue a hopeless marriage. It would not do to have a heroine benefit materially from a lapse in moral decorum. None of James's heroes do. Isabel's decision follows one of the most sensual passages found anywhere in his novels, in which Isabel experiences a lover's, and her own, passion:

> She felt his arms about her and his lips on her own lips. His kiss was like white lightning, a flash that spread, and spread again, and stayed; and it was extraordinary as if, while she took it, she felt each thing in his hard manhood that had least pleased her, each aggressive fact of his face, his figure, his presence, justified of its intense identity and made one with this act of possession. So had she heard of those wrecked and under water following a train of images before they sink.[7]

Why does Isabel reject the opportunity for a passionate, vital relationship in favor of a lifeless marriage? Tanner explains that "in running from the metaphorical sea of Caspar's kiss to the actual doorway of the lighted house, Isabel is avoiding the thing that is not named, but is all the more present for that – adultery, and the absolute annihilation of forms that it would imply for her" (Tanner, 18).

Thomas Hardy's Sue Bridehead knew all there was to know about the customs of love and marriage. In *Jude the Obscure* (1896), Hardy reverses some time-honored literary conventions. In Victorian fiction, frankness about sexual desire and action excluded marriage. Marriage had to do with "love," and "love" came to seem far removed from sexual satisfaction. In *Man and Woman: A Study of Love and the Novel, 1740-1940,* A. O. J. Cockshut notes that in most novels written by Hardy's predecessors, such as Swinburne and Thackeray, one would be led "to suppose that sexual desire, even sexual awareness, was something shared out between men and immodest women. Good girls and good wives were exempt."[8]

In his last novel, *Jude the Obscure,* Hardy sets out to subvert these assumptions. He makes the in-wedlock wife, Arabella, earthy, full figured, and elemental. He makes the mistress, Sue, angelic, intelligent, and prone to write off sex as crudely unworthy of her attention. Arabella traps Jude into marriage by a seductive ruse, followed by a deception about a bogus pregnancy. Cockshut finds Hardy's attempts to discredit marriage flawed.

> Hardy is more bound than he knows by the convention he is attacking. Arabella's carnality is treated as repulsive. It is not always easy to disentangle the different principles by which she is condemned. . . . Her open sexual invitation to Jude of wife to husband is clearly regarded as an obscenity. Yet, it could well be argued that since marriage is a sexual relationship, Arabella, for all her vices, . . . is more in harmony with the spirit of marriage *in this respect* than her rival Sue is. [Hardy] conceives himself to be showing that marriage is a fraud, since wives may be coarsely physical and sexually provocative. Actually, he is showing that he himself is really very like the literary predecessors he is supposed to be refuting. He finds it shocking that a wife should have the slightest interest in sex. (Cockshut, 126)

If Cockshut is right that Hardy's sense of the sexually fastidious Victorian wife reflects rather than counters the prevailing unwritten law that wives should be less carnal than mistresses, it is interesting that nearly all of the adulterous husbands in Alison Lurie's novels follow some such unwritten code. Brian Tate complains that Erica is unwilling to make love when or as he likes. "The truth is that sexual novelty has never been Erica's forte. The suggestion that she wear her new lace bra or her patent-leather boots to bed, or assume some unusual position, is apt to provoke suspicion" (*The Tates*, 46). Brian's lust for Wendy Gahaghan, the graduate student who will become his mistress, is fueled by his sense that, while with Erica nothing goes, with Wendy everything and anything goes. Sex with Erica "was further marred for Brian by the persistent image of Wendy Gahaghan lying on his office linoleum – exposed, silent, willing. . . . She was not similarly wary of innovation" (*The Tates*, 46-47).

In four of Lurie's first five novels, climaxed by Erica's counter-infidelity against Brian, the wives, viewed by their husbands as unsatisfactory in bed, discover in extramarital affairs a capacity for passionate sex unknown even to themselves.

Many fictional husbands cannot find the words – let alone the capability – to account for their dissatisfactions in the nuptial bed. H. G. Wells, whose "*terrible* fluidity of self-revelation" Henry James excoriated, cannot endow his usually articulate spokesman George Ponderevo with the candor to call his wife frigid. In *Tono-Bungay* (1908), though less poetical than George Eliot in *Middlemarch*, Wells similarly skirts the issue: "Who can tell the story of the slow estrangement of two married people, the weakening of first this bond and then that of that complex contract? Least of all can one of the two participants."[9]

It is to the anatomizing of nuptial estrangement that four of Alison Lurie's first five novels are devoted. In these books she proves herself the picker nonpareil of the lock in wedlock.

Chapter Three

Skirmishes on the Way to War

Four of Alison Lurie's first five novels can be grouped together, a tetralogy of tensions – mostly marital – that demoralize their heroines. Lurie has witnessed the dismantling of marriage both in her own life and in the lives of friends. Her women are almost always, like herself, well educated, sophisticated members of the upper-middle class. When their stories begin, these married protagonists appear to have reason for complacency. "Attractive and privileged," as Katharine M. Rogers points out, "they are successfully married to successful men [and have] . . . high moral standards. Having accepted the feminine mystique of the fifties, they devote themselves wholly to their families and expect marriage and children to provide them with happiness and fulfillment" (Rogers, 116-17). Lurie's tetralogy, beginning with *Love and Friendship* and concluding with *The War between the Tates,* while sharing what Rogers terms "this adultery plot," explores in varying ways her themes of marital discord and female consciousness raising.

Love and Friendship

Alison Lurie's first published novel may be most important for what it foretold. *Love and Friendship* (1962) presents in Emily Turner the first exhibit in what has become a fictional gallery of wives of academe who, although reluctant at first, eventually participate wholeheartedly in rites of infidelity. When Lurie declares in the novel's opening sentence that Emily fell out of love with her husband on a day like any other, she uses a matter-of-fact tone that characterizes this novel and three of the four that followed over the next dozen years. Emily Turner *(Love and Friendship),* Katharine Cattleman *(The Nowhere City),* Janet Belle Smith *(Real People),* and Erica Tate *(The War between the Tates)* have become disillusioned in their marriages, disenchanted by the men with whom they once, with utter confidence, exchanged vows.

Patches of light are allowed to break up the bleak domestic landscape. These women do have choices available to them that, while inimical to traditional concepts of marriage, enable them to experience previously unknown freedom – at least within themselves. Rogers describes the situation in which Lurie places such women:

> Typically, Lurie sets up alternatives in the form of the heroine's husband and a lover. Such a choice is realistically momentous for these women, who are committed not only to firm and conventional moral principles but to a confident belief that they are happily married. But, at the same time, Lurie uses the lover symbolically to represent a radically different life-style and set of values. (116)

Lurie's heroine is the well-bred, presumably virginal graduate of the right finishing school, safely married to an up-and-coming academic. But she eventually falls so out of line with the marital tenure track that she must, against the odds, follow one of her own making.

The provocation for Emily Turner's departure from the track reveals her fundamental belief that a wife lives most fully when engrossed in her husband's career. Having toughed out still another day with no conversational partner more stimulating than her preschool son, Emily is shocked when her husband, a college English instructor, refuses to answer her question as to how his day has gone. What especially enrages Emily is his response to her irritation with him: is she having her period?

The repercussions are not long in coming. Emily takes up with Will Thomas, a sexually pluralistic composer-in-residence; gets herself enveloped in an impossible salvage operation involving a colleague of her husband's named Julian Fenn; and eventually returns to the nuptial fold, perhaps wiser but – characteristically in Lurie – no more fulfilled. The novel concludes with an end-of-term lawn party in which the Turners' son Freddy and the Julian and Miranda Fenns' three children play a version of blindman's buff.

> The children ran back and forth. Laughing and screaming, they bumped against each other, bounced apart, waved their arms, and fell singly or in couples on the grass.
> "Freddy!" she called. He did not hear.

> Something was wrong with the game, though. "But they're all blind-folded!" Emmy objected.
> "Yes," Miranda said. "They like it better that way."[1]

Certainly Holman Turner qualifies as, if not blind, at least unseeing. Emily objects when Miranda comments about Holman,

> "It must be pleasant to be married to someone you can depend on . . . [Holman] always behaves so well to everybody. I was watching him at the Bakers' cocktail party."
> " . . . You only see him in public." But her sense of justice protested. "Of course, heavens, I don't mean he behaves badly in private. But he doesn't keep up his company manners. He's always so preoccupied when he's at home, he doesn't seem to notice Freddy or me or anything." She laughed a little nervously, unused to expressing this idea. (46)

For most of the book, Holman is portrayed as a cardboard husband. He pretends not to notice when Emily's sour mood persists for the whole semester. He can do nothing about women's ways. If her remarks, when they discuss Hum C, the Socratic course aimed at wiping each student's mental slate clean and for which Convers College is famous, always turn into self-analyses, well, Brian might ask, what could one expect of a woman? "She would always want to see every idea from an emotional point of view, if possible as an emotion; the class of things that had no connection with feeling did not interest her. He did not mind – *women should be that way"* (55, emphasis added). And, given her upper-middle-class New England background, that was the only way Emily *could* be. And he loves her that way. What he loves about her is that she is able to take order and beauty and abundance for granted, as if there was no other way to live. Holman never mentions these things for fear of breaking the spell.

He loved Convers College for similar reasons. Brought up in a Chicago neighborhood of rundown frame houses, the sight of pinecones fills him with much more happiness than did the jerry-built Christmas-tree decorations and green plastic wreathes of his childhood. He would like to share his ecstasy over the pinecones with his wife, but cannot. For them nothing is really shared.

Just as Emily Turner is a prototype for the Lurie heroine, Allen Ingram, a creative writing teacher at Convers who supplies the novel with much of its irony and wit through a series of letters, is an early model for the narrative voice that informs her later novels. Ingram, a homosexual writing to a lover, gives the novel the cutting, central intelligence that Lurie requires. Here, in the first of five novels with campus settings, her spokesperson catches exactly the right locution for the townpeople's disdain of academics. Ingram quotes a townswoman as saying, "They talk a lot up to the college"; then adds his own commentary, "But real life is going on somewhere else." He closes his late-winter letter: "It occurred to me that all of us college people here are like the snow, a cold white layer on top of the hot earth; superficial and, in the long run, probably temporary" (160).

The importance of Ingram's letters from Convers to his friend Francis Noyes in Greenwich Village cannot be overestimated. Inserted by Lurie as a sort of coda to each of the 17 chapters, they add a fresh consciousness, a kind of fringe intelligence, physically close to the action but far enough removed by temperament and bias to judge it by nonacademic standards. "My tourist's position gives me, perhaps, the necessary interested detachment," writes Ingram early in the book (76). The wry voice of Allen Ingram is the soul of an interest that is essentially disinterested. Following are some examples:

On a nonconformist, about-to-be-fired professor (Julian Fenn):

What [the administration] can't stand is his being such a queer fish/duck (what's so queer about ducks and fishes, I ask you?) He has Dirty Nails and Wears His Hair Too Long and Doesn't Own a Car and Rides His Bicycle for Miles in the Rain and Snow for No Conceivable Reason. . . . But what is [a successful career] but the proof that one has come to terms with society? (96)

On Fenn's firing:

[He] has officially been fired – or rather, as they say here, *let go*. The euphemism is really more accurate. *Fired* suggests circuses and cannons; you will get a much better picture of what's happened if you imagine a man hanging off a cliff on the end of a rope. With a shrug, the people at the other end *let go*. (135)

On the Turners:

She is a big, noisy, good-looking provincial deb . . . the serious, enthusiastic Bryn Mawr type of deb . . . better luck than Mr. Turner deserves, especially when you realize that she must have brought him a good deal of $$. . . . I am positive he comes from absolutely Nowhere. I feel a certain sympathy for Mrs. T–maybe fellow feeling because she and I come from somewhat the same background and we have both declassed ourselves by getting mixed up with the wrong sort of man? (181)

On Convers (early spring):

Truly, this place is death. Think of us all shut up in this narrow little valley, the interminable months of the northern winter. . . . By now everyone is sick or half insane or both. Will spring ever come? (205)

Of one of his students, a homosexual:

How does anyone in this world manage to reach 18 without having any, anything happen to him At all? So many of these Convers boys are . . . absolutely untouched. When I think what I went through . . . at thirteen, with Mother's second divorce and that episode at Newport the day of the boat race which, although (or because) I was in the main a spectator, certainly marked me for life. (224)

When Julian Fenn finally lands a position at Princeton, Ingram's observations issue straight from a maxim by LaRochefoucauld: "After all, it's hard enough to swallow a friend's good fortune, let alone an enemy's. Even Fenn's well-wishers are a bit abacktaken . . . – they never wished him quite *that* well" (244).

The perverse voice of Allen Ingram is subsumed in Lurie's later, more complex novels by an above-stage monitor who is all knowing and wise without the leveling drag of identity. But for now, in a first published novel, Ingram's epistolary voice foreshadows the more fully developed narrative voice characterizing later novels. A satirical novelist of substance has been born.

The Nowhere City

When Emily reunites with Holman in Lurie's first novel, it is only out of an ideal of self-sacrifice. That ideal, espoused early among New England heroines such as Isabel Archer and Hester Prynne, began to fray with Penelope Lapham in William Dean Howells's *The Rise of Silas Lapham* (1885). Penelope refuses to give up her requited love for Corey in favor of her sister, Irene, who happened to meet Corey first. The Laphams' minister praises Penelope for putting into practice an "economy of pain."[2] He demands that Silas's rigidly conventional wife Persis explain why it is better for three to suffer than one and states that "we are all weakened by a false ideal of self-sacrifice" (*Lapham*, 258). Emmy Turner, however, is not ready to abandon one kind of pain – self-sacrifice – for another – Holman's ruined career.

> He had to stay on [at Convers], and it would be frightfully important to him that there should be no . . . scandal. He could say now that she was visiting her parents, and then that they had agreed to a temporary separation. And then later he could let it quietly get about that there had been a divorce, and maybe later still . . . that she had remarried. That was how he would like it, that was what he would care about – much more than he would care about losing her. If it weren't for the scandal . . . he would probably be just as glad to be rid of her. (*L&F*, 305)

Emily Turner is reincarnated as Katherine (Mrs. Paul) Cattleman in *The Nowhere City* (1965). Although initially subject to the same notions of self-sacrifice as Emily, she is spared Emily's sentence to boring faculty wifedom by an accident of geography. Writing of Oakland, California, Gertrude Stein complained that "there is no *there* there."[3] Lurie's Los Angeles, unlike her Convers, is also a "no there" kind of city. Los Angeles has no moral presence; anything goes, and everything conspires to corrupt innocence. In Paul Cattleman's formulation, as he prepares to "make it" with a cool, Beckett-reading waitress named Ceci O'Connor, *Walden* has turned into *The Waste Land*, private pastoral into public lust.

Paul, a young historian sent West to spend a year writing the history of the Nutting Electronics Corporation, and Katherine, his New England-reared wife of four years who has unwillingly followed him, find themselves strangers in a strange land. *The Nowhere City* is the story of how Paul and Katherine, released from the conventions of the East, find themselves and lose their marriage.

Lurie complicates her adultery plot by involving not just the wife, as in *Love and Friendship*, but also the husband in infidelity. Paul had been unfaithful even before they moved West. Katherine labors under the handicap of a fidelity that borders on the compulsive. In everything, her rectitude is unassailable. She construes right action as necessarily abrogating self-interest to an ideal that is far beyond anything Don Quixote sought to defend.

She takes a job doing delinquency research in the UCLA Psychology Department because two of her three bosses fulfill her prescription for all men. They are "reasonable, predictable, and considerate of her."[4] Deliverance from her emotional straitjacket comes only when the third – a psychiatrist of Eastern European Jewish origin named Isadore Einsam – proves unreasonable, unpredictable, and inconsiderate in seducing her.

There is, of course, a danger in a novel so crammed with seductions that it may lapse into tabloid fiction. Lurie does not escape this peril. The argot of Venice Beach, with its "cool chicks," "big pads," "weird scenes," and "new gigs," used generously throughout the book, cannot alone evoke its world. "The bedroom scenes [with Paul and Ceci] are monotonous and the beatnik scenes implausible," charges an anonymous reviewer for the *London Times Literary Supplement.* "Miss Lurie's writing throughout is edged with a faint academic distaste, as if she were an able and literate inspector reporting on an eccentric progressive school."[5]

What is missing in *The Nowhere City* is the monitorial voice, above the slumming and the din, that would allow a satirical perspective. We have heard such a voice provided in Allen Ingram's letters from the Convers underground in *Love and Friendship.*

What does Alison Lurie expect her readers to make of the beatnik princess Ceci and her collection of free souls? Married to a half-Chinese exterminator salesman named Walter Wong, she only sleeps with her friends and, except for all those "squares" in the "other" culture, she hasn't an enemy in the world. After becoming a participant in one of Ceci's revels, Paul awakens to overhead projections out of Dali. If this were the ceiling of some decadent capitalist, Paul might have expected a mirror. But with Ceci's fantastic mural, he looks up to a man with a bird's head, lizards with wings, a dog with an electric toaster for a body.

It will be several months and some 200 pages before Paul will truly wake up. Once Ceci dashes Paul's illusions of an underground commune ("You mean [you want] a club of people who cheat on cats and chicks they're supposed to be making it with?") and mercifully terminates their affair ("Don't you know when something is over?"), he begins to think he will after all take a postdoctoral appointment at Convers College (the same Convers of *Love and Friendship*). He fails in his attempt to resume his relationship with

Katherine, now changed from her experience with Einsam. "I like you the way you are," Paul winces. To her offer of, in all senses, new positioning, he can only reply, "I don't want you to learn any techniques" (261).

But she has learned new techniques – and more. Full credit for the lyrical and ecstatic sexual experience that delivers Katherine from bondage to a stultifying marriage goes to Dr. Isadore (Iz) Einsam, Katherine's exuberant employer and aggressive lover, the novel's most interesting character. Mincing neither words nor intentions, Iz breaks through Katherine's defenses:

> "I'm sorry," Iz said in a not-sorry voice. "But I've never let any woman make a fool of me twice." With his free hand he took hold of Katherine's hair at the back of her neck, and turned her face forcibly towards his. "I'll tell you what I'm going to do." He spoke in a friendly, reasonable tone, almost as if he were dictating a report. " . . . Don't play coy with me. If you won't take your clothes off, I'll tear them off. If you won't lie down, I'll knock you down. If you won't make love to me, I'll rape you." (220)

Katherine is not violated in this scene. What is violated is her self-image as upholder at any cost of a bad marriage. She has been giving up everything for Paul in a grudging, painful way. The sinus headaches, about which she has complained since arriving in California, are the price of chronic self-sacrifice.

Iz Einsam is a catalyst for Katherine's passage to a new self-hood, but she recognizes the limits of the affair: "He was too much the guide. . . . After all, to stay with your doctor too long is to confess your illness chronic. If cured, you paid the bill and went away" (304). Iz suggests that their affair was a vacation trip for her, something outside "real life."

Besides, Iz is already married to a Hollywood starlet. Glory Green is all glitz, an actress whose face, even when she's on vacation, is "painted chalky brown all over, as if with Kemtone"(33). Glory issues straight from central casting, a Marilyn Monroe clone who, inexplicably, has a one-night stand with Paul Cattleman and briefly considers joining him in Convers. While she doesn't, like Monroe, express a desire to play Grushenka in *The Brothers Karamazov*, she does play sex-kitten-with-hidden-intellect when she laments to Paul, "Shit, you don't know how much I want to meet some real, serious, intellectual people, professors and thinkers . . . talking about serious things, like art and philosophy "(299). For a moment, Paul imagines Glory Green in her pink bathing suit at a Convers gathering. The Cattlemans do not divorce in the book, but their marriage is over. Paul returns from a trip to Convers to find a note from Katherine that she has gone to a reunion party for Iz and his Glory. Paul attends the party, where he notices "a pretty girl in tight yellow pants, with a smooth California tan and ash-blonde hair piled up on her head like a mound of whipped cream; an obvious Los Angeles type [whom] he remembered vaguely seeing . . . earlier" (332-33). He fails to realize that this woman is Katherine.

When Paul leaves Los Angeles for good, Katherine does not drive him to the airport. She remains in the city where, as she saw from the start, whatever happens does not count.

Real People

Writer Lester Goldberg credits Alison Lurie's fourth novel, *Real People* (1969), for his resolution never to write a story that proceeds like this: "I am a writer who is writing this story who may not be writing this story who is a writer who knows the first writer who is writing about the second writer and so on."[6] Can there be much interest in novels about writers writing about writers writing?

Unpromising as such fictional material would appear to be, the question can only be answered by another: Has Lurie found ways to generate life from Janet Belle Smith's journal entries of a week-long stay at a northern New England artists' retreat, Illyria (read Yaddo, Saratoga Springs, New York, where Lurie held several visitorships during the 1960s)?

At face value, Janet in her diary seems sensitive but frequently sententious, diffident yet determined. She hopes her observations of the others at the retreat are funny as well as shrewd. But Janet should not be taken at face value. She belongs to the tradition of the unreliable narrator. Readers can no more take Janet on her own terms than they can someone like Dowell in Ford Madox Ford's *The Good Soldier* or Dostoevski's Underground Man in *Notes from Underground*.[7] The richness of a book like *Real People* lies beneath the surface of the first-person narration.

Janet Belle Smith, 42, is enduring something like writer's block although six months earlier she had published a book of stories. Her husband, Clark, an insurance executive, considers her writing a hobby, like bird watching, and cannot understand why she continues to pursue something that "seems to cause mainly discomfort."[8] Janet, who has inserted *Belle* between given name and surname to add euphony to the prosaic, believes that at "Illyria one becomes one's *real* self, the person one would be in a decent world" (17, emphasis added).

As with most of Lurie's book titles, *Real People* is ironic. "Real" and "reality," words that Vladimir Nabokov declares should never be written without quotation marks, must be sorted out by Janet, both outside and inside the writer's world. Characteristically, Lurie assigns a key observation to a child, when a little boy's voice breaks free from a group of tourists visiting Illyria, "Are those artists, Mom, or are they real people?" (53).

The progress of *Real People* becomes Janet's gradual triumph over the sophisticated impersonality with which she writes her journal. For two-thirds of the book, she combines patches of remembered dialogue, shorthand ideas for stories, usually having to do with ghosts, and the fitting of the other guests into tableaux that she can dominate through false-sounding solicitude. Except for *Imaginary Friends*, *Real People* is Lurie's only novel written in the first person. Her choice was a wise one. As Rogers puts it, Lurie's use of the first person "directly involves us in Janet's self-deception and the unpleasant self-recognition that follows" (Rogers, 120).

No Lurie heroine can "come clean" with herself without the crucible of a seduction. Shocking the seemingly impervious Janet out of her self-deception requires an antagonist who is taken in neither by art for talk's sake nor by Janet's facade. Nick Donato, a sexy junk sculptor, proves that opposites attract. He plays Benedick hoping for a Beatrice beneath the layers of pretense.

Nick begins by commenting on Janet's preference in conversation for *one* over *I* ("Janet has an imaginary friend named Wun. An Oriental. She's always telling us his opinions. Wun prefers the kind of art Wun was brought up on. Wun is responsible, after all"[75].) He breaks through her defenses by confronting her with a fact she doesn't want to face: Kenneth Foster, a painter with whom she has a platonic friendship, is a homosexual. "Shit, Janet, I'm not trying to put Foster down. I've got nothing against queers" (*Real People*, 98). When she goes to bed with Nick it is not so much a reward to him as an act of certification for the woman to be.

Rogers makes clear the importance of Nick to Janet's awakening to the *real* claims of self:

> She leaves after a passionate encounter that makes her *recognize* impulses in her that do not at all fit her refined self-image: she not only has a strong sexuality, but has responded to a man who violates all her standards. . . . Nick [also] makes her *see* the truth about her genteel substitute for adultery and her compromise between niceness and artistic expression: Kenneth did not abstain from sexual overtures out of consideration and respect for her but because, as a homosexual, he was not interested; she cannot be a serious writer if she insists on censoring herself in order to maintain everyone's approval. (120, emphasis added)

The key words are *recognize* and *see*. Nick's wounding candor has brought Janet from ignorance to self-knowledge – to something Aristotle codified as Recognition. Now her self-satisfaction, which masqueraded as diffidence, will no longer, to use a favorite Lurie metaphor, clothe her for the outside world and herself. The diary form, in Lurie's special use of it, charts for the reader the changes in Janet as she experiences them.

H. Porter Abbott, in *Diary Fiction: Writing As Action*, places *Real People* as the centerpiece in a key chapter, "The Special Reflexive Function of Diary Strategy." From the point where Janet takes off her blinders as well as her clothes, she begins to rewrite all the most crucial aspects of her story as she had earlier recorded it. "The text corrects itself," writes Professor Abbott. "In other words, our enlightenment about [Nick Donato and Ken Foster] . . . roughly keeps pace with the enlightenment of our narrator."[9]

Janet has evolved from a "charming, intelligent, sensitive lady writer who lives in a nice house . . . with her nice family, and never makes any serious mistakes or has any real problems" (*Real People*, 152). She has become someone capable of "true writing," which George Orwell, in the midst of completing *Nineteen Eighty-Four*, defined as "the product of the saner self that stands aside, records the things that are done and admits their necessity, but refuses to be deceived as to their true nature."[10]

The foregoing should not give the impression that her conversion is immediate. At first, Janet tries to sublimate her tryst with Nick into the plot of a ghost story. But, to the diary that has heard her earlier confession, she makes another.

There was something in the original ideas, but then I changed the people to types, and the precipitating incident from a seduction to news of a death. Which is of course more conventional for a ghost story, less apt to surprise or offend anyone – and also isn't what I want to write about. I'm tired of ghosts – whether they're real "spirits" or just spiritualized versions of myself and the people I know. (125)

Discarding protective fantasy in her diary helps Janet to drop pretense in her life. She, who in an earlier entry "was never going to [Nick's] studio again," does indeed go – and with the same result.

The final pages of *Real People* are devoted to a colloquy between Janet and Kenneth. Janet sets down their words like a dialogue in a play, just as she has done before, except that by now the reader credits her entries as honest. Ken tells Janet he knows about her affair with Nick, but he disappoints her by withholding anger. Instead, he faults her for the priggish and self-satisfied character of her behavior and her writing. Their parting, like their relationship, is mild and inoffensive, just as it had always been. Janet consoles herself in believing that everything Ken said issued not from regard for her but from jealousy, spite, and disappointment. "Because his lovely Janet doesn't really exist and never did, any more than my lovely Kenneth. They were both just ghosts in some story we were telling each other and ourselves. Very charming and spiritual, like all ghosts, but in the end thin, transparent and boring" (156).

Alison Lurie received Yaddo Foundation fellowships for 1963, 1964, and 1966. One should not be tempted to equate Lurie with the heroine of *Real People*, with whom she may share some professional and domestic interests. Lurie asserts that her heroines have tie-ins to her but that none is the autobiographical self. Especially illuminating in this connection is "No One Asked Me to Write a Novel," in which she discusses her awakening as a writer in terms that Janet Belle Smith would recognize. After twice trying to break the habit of writing, she credits the memory of her prematurely dead friend, Bunny Lang, and the subsequent writing of Lang's story as producing "a series of flashes of light" whose effect had much in common with Janet's resurgence.

Lurie writes that she worked without caring or worrying "about whether my sentences would please some editor." While recognizing that what she wrote "wasn't the whole truth – I couldn't know that – it was part of the truth, my truth. I could still cast spells, reshape events" ("No One Asked," 47).

Liberated, like Janet, "to use everything in her art, including hate and envy and lust and fear" (*Real People,* 157), Alison Lurie threw every resource at her command into the writing of her next book, *The War between the Tates*.

Chapter Four

The War between the Tates

War as Domestic Metaphor

No contemporary account better evokes the nature of university life in the embattled 1960s than Alison Lurie's fifth novel, *The War between the Tates* (1974). Warfare, domestic and overseas, was the violent touchstone of the period. War is the dominant metaphor of the novel. Lurie writes:

> The war in Southeast Asia is escalating, and Jones Creek is polluted with detergent.
>   At home everything is falling apart. Most obviously the children whose early adolescent rebellion, instead of running its course, has been *escalating*. (94, emphasis added)

Her use in an unlikely context of *escalating*, a State Department buzzword, anticipates the novel's game-plan. Erica and Brian Tate are at war on the homefront, too, and the conduct of that war—its mercurial, nobody-wins tactics—perfectly reflects the larger war.

Although cease-fire for the Tates, fittingly enough, comes during a peace march, Lurie rarely brings the actual war into the action. But the war does provide a book-long conceit. The progress of *The War between the Tates* mirrors the progress of most military actions. The reader is witness, in the lives of the Tates and their friends, to the declaration of war, the recruitment of allies, and the marshalling of commanders and troops. We see the intricacies of espionage and the complex deployment of tactics sometimes from the frontline and sometimes from a distant vantage point. Vitally important skirmishes between some of the contenders are left unrecorded, as in the chaos of war itself, when smoke, shouts, and fear distort and destroy communication.[1]

At the end of the Vietnam War America sought an elusive peace with honor. At the end of their long year's hostilities, perhaps the Tates could say, like Falstaff *in King Henry IV,* that "honor is a mere scutcheon."[2] If Lurie cannot confer intactness – let alone honor – at the end of the Tates' war, she does allow them something toward which her earlier couples merely groped: mutual understanding.

Erica Tate

What Katharine M. Rogers calls "Lurie's breaking marriage plot" culminates in *The War between the Tates* (Rogers, 122). Now, for the first time in her fiction of adultery, the promissory notes are paid in full. What for Emily Turner in *Love and Friendship* had become a husband who seemed more and more like a stranger she didn't especially like becomes for Erica Tate a selfish deceiver ready to jeopardize a satisfying career and "perfect" marriage for an affair with a pitiable hippie graduate student. What for Katherine Cattleman in *The Nowhere City* had been passed off as the deleterious effect of southern California culture becomes a savage indictment of middlebrow marital rites and an exposé of the effects of implicit bad faith between partners.

It is Erica Tate's false sense of noblesse oblige that is under assault here. That assault began when Erica was 10 years old, when her father ran off and her mother had to work in a store. It recurs during the cold spring morning on which the novel opens.

Erica is a 39-year-old housewife and mother, Radcliffe graduate, and the author and illustrator of three children's books concerning the adventures of an ostrich named Sanford. Living as the Tates do in one of the ice-box regions of the country, Erica is used to March going out as it came in – like a lion. But this morning, on the last day of winter, she "feels her emotional temperature, which has been unnaturally low of late, rise several degrees" (*The Tates,* 3). She shares the news that spring begins tomorrow with her son, Jeffrey (Jeffo), but he only complains that there are no sausages to go with the eggs. Erica's daughter, Matilda (Muffy), is equally unresponsive to her mother's ebullient mood, but she complains that there is too much for breakfast ("I can't eat this stuff. It's fattening".) Moreover, the irritating noise of bulldozers, readying the adjacent property for still another ranch house, remind Erica of what she views as the deterioration of their neighborhood. She desperately looks for solace from Jeffo or Muffy; their lack of interest strikes her as cold and uncaring. If only her husband, Brian, were here, but he is lecturing on foreign policy at Dartmouth. Euphoria gives way to a nagging misanthropy, and Erica loses her composure: "You don't care what's happening to our road!" she cries. "How can you be so selfish, so unfeeling? You don't really mind at all, either of you" (4)! The building of expensive but gauche new homes is threatening Erica's identity. Even worse, the children do not care. At one time, perfectly reflecting Erica and Brian's ideals, they would have cared.

Heroines in nineteenth-century novels often meet crises with deep self-examination. After late-night vigils, at least two – George Eliot's Dorothea Brooke in *Middlemarch* and Henry James's Isabel Archer in *The Portrait of a Lady* – vowed, mind over heart, to go on. But neither had children to complicate the picture. Erica Tate falls to sobbing over the breakfast dishes. She owns up to a positive dislike of her children. Long before Lurie has posted the bulletin that closes the chapter – "The war has begun" – we know that none of the old accommodations sensitive women have traditionally made to the establishment, in fiction and in life, will do for Erica.

We learn early in the novel that there is reason for Erica's alienation of affections. Lurie, employing an analogy from Cold-War philosopher George Kennan,[3] portrays Erica as forever doomed to an "area of operations" that makes her – and her alone – responsible for the children.

An admirer of George Kennan's early writings, [Brian] had long subscribed to the doctrine of separate spheres of influence, both in national and domestic matters; he attributed the success of their marriage partly to this doctrine. He might advise Erica on important policy decisions, but ordinarily he would not question her management of the home, nor would she ever try to intervene in his professional life. If he lost his job (which had never been very likely and was now impossible, since he had tenure), it was his fault. If the children became uncontrollable, it was hers. (8)

Danielle Zimmern, a former Radcliffe classmate of Erica who also married an academic, offers an interesting counterpoint as man-hating divorcée to Erica's ultimate faithfulness to Brian. Erica and Danielle had avoided each other at Radcliffe "for the same motive that prevents Atwater's Supermarket from placing cases of ice cream and sherbert next to cartons of beer. But now that they had both been purchased and brought home, this ceased to matter" (12). Erica's and Danielle's marriages to Ivy League academics had united them. Their daughters, Muffy and Ruth, are inseparable, their husbands, Brian and Leonard, close friends. (Leonard is the insufferable 14-year-old Lennie in *Only Children* and the acerbic L. D. Zimmern in *Foreign Affairs*. See the appendix for a discussion of the evolution of this character in Lurie's novels.)

The Zimmerns, unlike the Tates, opt for divorce in the face of marital distress. "It was as if [the Tates and the Zimmerns] were actively supporting rival parties, Marriage and Divorce, but had agreed not to discuss politics," Lurie writes (15). Divorce is not an option for Lurie's protagonists in this novel or in any other. Erica's ultimate decision to stay with Brian has proven problematic for a number of critics, as will be discussed shortly.

Brian Tate

Even before Wendy Gahaghan breezes into his seminar and into his life, Brian Tate believes "that his appearance is the objective correlative of a lack of real stature" (33). Not only Erica but his dream of becoming a great man tower well above his reach. His is that kind of local success he secretly despises. At 46, he holds an endowed chair in the political science department at Corinth University, the kind that carries little salary increase and no reduction in teaching load. When he lectures on foreign policy or publishes a profitable textbook, his students and colleagues are reminded of his success; he is reminded of his failure. Like Mr. Ramsay in Virginia Woolf's *To the Lighthouse*, Brian was among the very few who reach Q-level, but would never make it to R—and knew it. Why, Brian "asks himself sourly, is he speaking on foreign policy instead of helping to make it? Why does he still discuss other men's theories instead of his own" (31)?

Only once has Erica even hinted that Brian has disappointed her. After a party in New York, at which several celebrities were present, she pulled her petticoat over her dark curls and said she would like her husband to be famous, too. Until Wendy, she extolled their privacy, which would be lost if Brian were to become more prominent.

Brian basks in the illusion that he is as misunderstood as his hero, George Kennan, the philosopher of the Cold War. As noted by Judie Newman, three terms of key significance in Kennan's thought have application in *The War between the Tates:* "He made his name with the 'containment' doctrine of the 1940s, became the advocate of 'disengagement' in the 1950s and spoke out in the 1960s against global interventionism (e.g., in Vietnam) and in favor of *détente* and 'neo-isolationism' " (Newman, 105). Brian, like his hero, is ultimately regarded as fuzzy minded, small minded, or both. "Making it" with Wendy, as she puts it, will be both the breaking and the remaking of him. Brian applies all sorts of theories to this most entangling of alliances, but none improve on the following:

> He needed [Wendy] to quiet the anxiety that he was in every sense, including the most private, a small man. In a shady part of his mind which he did not usually visit he wished to learn [Erica's] opinion on this matter. Erica could not judge it, any more than she could judge his professional competence, since, having known no other men, she had no means of comparison. . . . Brian recognized the childish neurotic stupidity of these ideas, but he could not suppress them. . . . "Just once; just one shot, that's all, to cure you both," his addiction whispered; and at last he promised it what it wanted. (48)

Like Ceci, Paul Cattleman's lover in *The Nowhere City,* Wendy is a caricature – a "quite marvelous" one, according to Phoebe Adams, in whom "Ms. Lurie has managed to fit together, in one awful wench, every characteristic that has ever maddened a college administrator."[4] In fact, it may be that Wendy's lack of popularity, so much in contrast with his wife's popularity at Wendy's age, adds to her appeal. Brian "would have been on his guard if she had been anything like his wife at that age. But Erica had been exceptional . . . one of the most popular girls in her class – always surrounded by admirers and friends" (38).

Julian Jebb, however, finds Lurie's treatment of Wendy "a damaging element to the subtle moral and comic balance of the book."[5] Since, with an array of British critics, Jebb is a devoted fan of Lurie's, his single disclaimer bears notation: "To all the other characters Miss Lurie extends what might be described as a concealed warmth – a belief that for all their moral failures she likes them. The appalling children; her hypocrite husband; her sluttish friend Danielle . . . each possess – or have possessed – radiant saving graces. Though she tries, Miss Lurie fails to be just to Wendy" (Jebb, 127).

Jebb goes on to decry Lurie's hatred of Wendy's mindless devotion to Brian, her degradation of language, and her pursuance of the unexamined life. (Overall, nonetheless, the review is both generous and searching. Jebb commends Lurie's "fearlessness": "Vonnegut, Updike, Mailer, Philip Roth may lay claim to greater literary inventiveness – but none of them tell their truth with the sophisticated directness of Alison Lurie. . . . There are no lies in *The War between the Tates*" [Jebb, 128].)

Countering the Counterculture

In a 1985 interview in Dallas published in the *Southwest Review* the next year, Alison Lurie observes that she likes "to have at least two stories going at once because they can play off each other, and I don't think any one story can say everything about the world."[6] Although she was responding to a question about the double plot of *Foreign Affairs*, Lurie does use the Tates as sounding boards for one another. At the same time, on a larger stage, the novel offers two attitudes or sensibilities in counterpoint to each other – the pre-1960s, tradition-bound sensibility of the Tates and their peers and the contemporary, rebellious sensibility of the characters representing the counterculture: feminists (like Danielle), would-be free souls (like Wendy), turned-off mystics (like Zed, proprietor of Krishna Books and Erica's ambivalent lover), and protesters (like the student marchers). The Tates, faced with middle-age and an attendant winding down of self-illusions, are at once drawn to and repelled by these characters. Michael S. Helfand, in the only essay to address the necessarily fragmented viewpoints of the Tates, explains:

> For both Tates, fantasies are punctured by social realities. The pious Liberalism of Brian and Erica masks their envy of the youthful communal, mystical and uninhibited life of the counter-culture communities, the life style which they repressed or lost to attain middle class respectability.
>
> . . . Feminism, mysticism and communal living represent the unacknowledged needs of the Tates. . . . It is left to the communal and "irrational"

Wendy . . . [and the other] honest folk in the counter-culture . . . to reveal the truth.[7]

The novel fluctuates between the Tates' recognition of the passing of their youth and its self-deception and their denial of this awareness, an inability to give up their image of themselves as perfect. In her previous novels, Lurie rarely resorted to the storyteller's trick of going beneath the surface of the action to obtain a reliable view of a character's mind and heart. Her use of an all-knowing narrator for the first time in *The War between the Tates* informs us of what no one in the "real life" of the novel could possibly know. To gain access to the larger war between truth and fantasy in the Tates, Lurie occasionally eschews social realism, which has served her well, for epiphanic moments. Two reveal her technique.

First, Brian: Pacing the hall of the Frick gallery, awaiting the always tardy Wendy, he sees both the virtues and defects of his new lifestyle away from Erica and the children.

Now that he has vacated it, Brian realizes he has been living in a hostile camp, among people who at best tolerated, at worst exploited and defied him, for a long time. . . . What amazes him most is that his discovery has come so late . . . forty-six years without knowing what it is to be really loved. . . .

As for Erica, Brian has always known that she cared less for him than he did for her. From the start he was the one who loved, while she allowed herself to be loved. That was her nature. . . . Brian could accept that . . . until he met Wendy, who never judges him, withholds nothing, cares more for him than for herself.

Of course this unconditional love has disadvantages. Sometimes Brian feels like a man with a new, over-affectionate pet, whose constant and obvious devotion is half a source of satisfaction, half an embarrassment. (208-9)

Brian is capable of such moments of awareness, but his learned responses ultimately lead him to distort authentic perception to conform to his egotistic illusions. In a moment, he will identify Wendy with a young woman in a painting of an "elegant pastoral love affair" titled *Reverie*.

Now, Erica: At Danielle's, before a party, she approaches a Victorian set of drawers and its wide mirror. Drawing close to the glass, she finds

there are shallow folds on either side of the generous mouth and between the dark brows but no wrinkles. But Danielle's body looks heavy, used. . . .
  Women age like wild apples, Erica read once. Most, fallen under the tree and ungathered, gradually soften and bulge and go brown and rotten; and that is what will happen to Danielle. Others hang on to the branch, where they wither and shrink and freeze as winter comes on. This is how it will be with her. (257-58)

In Sandy (Zed) Finkelstein, the owner of an occult bookstore who has worshipped her from afar since their graduate school days, Erica finds some reprieve from her struggles with Brian and the inevitability of aging. Unselfish and loving, he is the only character in the book who is not involved in competition or "war." Like Janet Smith of *Real People*, Erica is given an opportunity to grow through self-knowledge, but Erica is not up to it. As Rogers points out, although Erica "can now value [Zed's] freedom from convention and egotism and can recognize the wisdom of his saying that we must all some time adjust to being losers, she realizes that she needs the security and success that Brian offers" (Rogers, 121).

    In *Love and Friendship, The Nowhere City*, and *Real People* one can only conjecture whether divorce is in store for the protagonists. In *The War between the Tates*, Erica and Brian go as far as hiring attorneys. That they reconcile after so lacerating a "war" is, for Rogers, an indication of "Lurie's realistically disenchanted view of marriage; she recognizes that every match is a compromise in which, at best, people find those who meet their most important needs" (Rogers, 122).

    Late in *The War between the Tates*, Erica visits her divorced friend Danielle to discuss developments in her recent separation from Brian. But it is Danielle for whom she commiserates. Danielle's 14-year-old daughter, Roo, having learned how chickens are slaughtered, is a convert to vegetarianism. This revealing colloquy takes place:

"She told me this morning she can only have unfertile eggs for breakfast. Where the hell am I supposed to get unfertile eggs?" Danielle laughs.
    "I thought all eggs nowadays were unfertile," Erica says, trying hard not to think of Wendy's fertile egg.
    "So did I. But apparently not, at least not at the Co-op. . . . I can't keep up with her any more. The rules keep changing too fast."

> "... But that's how it is with everything. You know what I feel sometimes?" Erica adds. . . . "As if I'd got into a time machine, like in one of Jeffrey's science-fiction stories, and been shot forward into the wrong time. Nineteen sixty-nine – it doesn't sound right, it's a year I don't belong in. It doesn't even feel real. Reality was when the children were small, and before the housing development."
>
> "And before Lennie and Brian left home. Yeh. I know what you mean."
>
> "You see, we know all the rules for that world. . . . [but] everything's changed, and I'm too tired to learn the new rules. I don't care about nineteen sixty-nine at all. I don't care about rock festivals or black power or student revolutions or going to the moon. I feel like an exhausted time traveler. . . . These new developments . . . have nothing to do with real life." (237-38)

This excerpt reveals late in the war games Erica's spiritual base of operations, her feeling of being trapped in a time warp in which she can find no recognizable "reality." She will see the war through as a combatant and partake of its perquisites. She will even be the aggressor in a brief affair with a former admirer from her Radcliffe days, now 20 years behind her. But Zed cannot be long for her world.

Lurie, who recently faulted her friend David Lodge's satirical novel *Nice Work* (1989) for denying its characters – academics – a real kind of lyrical and ecstatic sexual experience, never withholds such possibilities from hers.[8] The love scenes with Zed (born Sanford Finkelstein, having dropped "Sanford" in deference to the ostrich by that name in Erica's children's books) and Erica bespeak a potentially idyllic relationship. Their first encounter, which takes place in Zed's Krishna bookstore, proves abortive but promising:

> At first it is hardly like being kissed at all; then Zed, with a clumsy, half-blind gesture, pulls her closer and shifts his mouth so that it meets hers more accurately. . . .
>
> But he only holds her, stroking her face and hair, kissing her gently and intermittently . . . but Zed releases her, blinking and putting out one hand to feel for the shelf behind him. (293)

Erica leaves, but not without an "idea of how large a present she intends to give him" (292-93).

Their second meeting, a carefully orchestrated assignation in her own house, finds Zed impotent but no less interested. The next, in her office late at night, goes little better sexually. Spiritually, however, the mystic scores. Zed argues that the human condition should be miserable everywhere–and equally–so that almost everyone would be sick and ugly and frightened and hungry. Only a few would be spared–to be scattered about to remind the miserable of what they were missing. "That's what people like you and Brian are for," he lashes out at Erica with unaccustomed severity (327).

Finally, Erica agrees to an LSD picnic with Zed at the abandoned apartment of one of his Zen students, and the two make love. At the close of their hallucinatory adventure, Zed discloses that he plans to leave Corinth and asks Erica to come with him. Erica's response is firmly traditional. She will not desert her children. She will seek a reconciliation with Brian.

The fate of Brian, while also predictable, is capped by perhaps the most ironically comic scene in any of Lurie's novels. During the brief period he lives with Wendy, Brian finds himself inadvertently aligned with Corinth's militant feminists. When Donald Dibble, his despised department chair, is exposed for his incendiary chauvinist lectures and made a prisoner of the feminists in his own office, Brian realizes he must "rescue" him, afraid that Dibble may not survive the ordeal because of his poor health. After springing Dibble with a crude rope ladder, Brian finds himself climbing out the window of the political science building pursued by an angry posse of feminists. While Dibble, the real culprit, will escape criticism–and probably land a better job–Brian has no alternative to remaining in Corinth where he has become–overnight–a national hero of reactionary antifeminism, with his photograph in newspapers coast to coast. After trying for 47 years, Brian Tate has become a famous man.

The likelihood of the Tates' reconciliation, especially given the tumultuousness of the 1960s, is questionable, and several prominent reviewers have faulted it. By allowing it, they say in effect, Lurie, novelistically, painted herself into a corner. The reconciliation means that the Tates' temporary lovers have to be dispatched like extra baggage.

Lurie's resolutions, however, are consistent with the times. The pregnant Wendy's innate decency combines with a commonplace of the 1960s–the open road–to provide her with a convincing exit. She will have Brian's child ("I couldn't ever desert a kid" [359]), but she will also end her pursuit of its father, in spite of a sympathetic reminder from Erica of the advantages of accepting Brian's proposal ("If you were to marry him, you'd have some security" [359]). Wendy and a new friend, Ralph, will shake the dust of academe in Corinth for a commune in California. If Jebb's contention is valid – if Wendy has been portrayed unsympathetically – Lurie does at the end endow her with something like wisdom. ("Once you're married you can't ever tell if the guy comes home on account of he wants to, or on account of he has to.")

Sandy makes a limp suggestion that Erica go away with him and for once give Brian a shot at taking care of the kids. Emerging from the LSD trip she has shared with him, Erica laughs nervously, thinks of herself as someone avoiding a precipice. She will do something at the start of the 1970s that the 1990s would install as a byword. She will do the right thing.

The final tableau is one of self-recognition and reconciliation for Brian and Erica:

> They will talk for a long while after lunch. . . . Moving into the sitting room – Erica curled on the blue sofa as usual, and he in his wing chair – they will relate and explain all that has passed. They will laugh, and possibly at some moments cry. They will encourage each other, console each other, and forgive each other. Finally, as the afternoon lengthens and the shadows of half-fledged trees reach toward the house, they will put their arms about each other and forget for a few moments that they were once exceptionally handsome, intelligent, righteous and successful young people; they will forget that they are ugly, guilty and dying. (371-72)

Roger Sale finds the passage, rich though it is, wrong for the book.[9] He wishes, for Erica, something more, something better. The outcome of the novel may be untrue to the era, even to the artistic integrity of the novel. It may be unworthy of Erica's potential. The ending is, however, true to personal history – specifically, Erica Tate's personal history – from which no one can escape.

In one of his prefaces Henry James says, "There are depths." He refers to the serious novelist's commitment to the psychological complexity of any worthwhile character. Isabel Archer ends her midnight vigil knowing that she cannot in good faith leave Gilbert Osmond, for she knows that he, too, has been let down in their marriage. Erica and Brian Tate are Alison Lurie's first couple to have "depths." They undergo trials, skillfully illumined by Lurie, and they reunite with fewer expectations but more understanding. Having considered – even enacted – other options and broken the constraints by which their lives had failed, they have emerged being capable of realistic compromise in the interest of survival.

Chapter Five

Subversions

Alison Lurie believes that childhood represents the last stronghold of decency and that children's literature offers access to values that have largely disappeared in adult society. To the first idea she has devoted a major novel, *Only Children* (1979); to the second, an impressive body of essays on children's literature that were collected and published recently as *Don't Tell the Grown-ups: Subversive Children's Literature* (1990).

In *Only Children* Lurie chooses sides in the struggle between the innocence of childhood and the corruption of the adult world. It appeared midway between her two best-known books, *The War between the Tates* and *Foreign Affairs*, a chronology that permits certain conjectures about life and art and the mandates of zeitgeist.

For Lurie to write about the Tates while experiencing the women's movement and the student protests of the 1960s in her own life as the wife of a university professor and the mother of three boys, two of whom were teenagers, presented difficulties. Lurie has always denied writing autobiographical fiction ("Some of my women share certain aspects but none is really like me," she told an interviewer.[1]) Richard Ellmann writes of James Joyce that "the fact that he was turning his life to fiction at the same time that he was living it encouraged him to feel a certain detachment from what [was happening] to him, for he knew he could reconsider and re-order it for the purposes of his book."[2] Perhaps it was that way with Lurie in composing *The War between the Tates*, with the tensions of the times setting the tone but not necessarily the order of events.

This much is sure, however: her decision to shift for the first time in a long narrative from the historic past tense to the present tense was determined by the way middle-class Americans like herself were living. "I needed a . . . journalistic immediacy of the kind that reports of the Vietnam War, the campus revolts as well as the reports of domestic wars are pitched to," she noted recently (Conversation).

When for *Only Children* she turned from the evocation of the immediate to the recovery of the past of childhood, a more formidable
narrative mandate presented itself.

Grown-ups' Subversion: *Only Children*

Because of her experience of family and motherhood, which she has
described as providing her surest novelistic footing, and her lifelong
commitment to the literature of children, Alison Lurie knows well
perhaps *the* salient truth about children. At the close of her review of
Only Children, Mary Gordon puts the matter well: "Children are
sentenced to live in the domestic world until they are old enough to
escape it. In *Only Children,* Lurie makes it clear why they want to
escape. Their safety there is temporary and uneven. The grown-ups
aren't always in charge."[3] The grown-ups in the novel are rarely in
charge of their world, and the children are trying to make sense of it.

In *Only Children,* Lurie divides what Henry James called
"centres" between two modes of experience. In those segments that
are viewed from adult vantage, Lurie employs the conventional
historical past tense. Almost no one soliloquizes; we are alerted to
the passing of time. Most of these chapters open with, and depend
on, exactly defined intervals ("As morning advanced, the sun swung
west over the Catskills, slanting into the front bedrooms of Anna's
house.").[4] When Lurie focuses on the two girls in the novel, Lolly
Zimmern and Mary Ann Hubbard, time is unheeded, creating the
sense of timelessness associated with childhood. The children are
immersed in their experience of the moment, as Lolly is in the
following passage: "All the dining room is filling up with noise and
words, loud frightened worried ones that don't melt away in the air
the way most words do, but bounce and crowd. Like the balloons of
words in comic strips, nudging and pushing, floating round Mr.
Hubbard and Anna and Mummy-Celia and Lennie, piled on the floor
and tables and chairs" (145).

Some years later, Lurie described J. M. Barrie's *Peter Pan* as
"much more than a conventional pantomime." Never-never land,
where there is no time, is "the world of childhood imagination . . . a
refuge from the adult universe of rules and duties."[5]

Only Children "is the most interior of Lurie's novels," writes Gordon (31). Her words pinpoint the book's place in the refining of Lurie's craft and the deepening of her art. In this novel, the time and place she chooses have a softer ambience than any previous work. The time is a Fourth-of-July weekend in 1935, in the midst of the Great Depression; the place a farm in the Catskill Mountains. A cast of eight follows a traditional format for comedy, the innocent spirit of roughing it in the country gradually stricken by problems – generational and sexual – at the heart of things.

The title can be interpreted at least three ways. Each reveals an interlocking facet of the book's message. It may be read as a suggestion that only children can bring right conduct into adult lives. It may convey the notion that grown-ups are only children, remaining childish without being childlike; this distinction is dramatized in the tension between corruption of innocence and its subtler corollary, innocence of corruption. Finally, the words of the title actually issue from Mary Ann's mother, Honey (Honoria) Hubbard. "After all," she says upon realizing that a violent row between the adults has been witnessed by the children, "they're only children" (*Only Children*, 240).

Alison Lurie's debt to Henry James will be discussed in the next chapter on *Foreign Affairs*. Like him, she knows the child's world to be a jigsaw puzzle, containing pieces of literal observation but lacking a complete picture. In James's *What Maisie Knew*, many serious matters are broached in Maisie's presence. In *Only Children*, the observations of two eight-year-old girls, Mary Ann and Lolly, constitute what James would have regarded as the novel's central intelligence. In his preface to *What Maisie Knew*, written a decade after original publication, James described Maisie's "small demonic foresight" as taking in "the rich little spectacle of objects embalmed in her wonder."[6] Both James's Maisie and Lurie's Mary Ann live rich imaginative lives.

It is Mary Ann's fantasy that frames the novel's five-day scenario. What was more conducive to day-dreaming in the 1930s than to be sitting in the back seat of one's parents' Franklin automobile en route to a long holiday weekend in the country? The people of Mary Ann's world include two contrasting couples. Mary Ann's mother, Honey, a preening southern belle, is called "kitten" by her husband, but she has never been declawed. Bill, Mary Ann's father, is a New

Deal Democrat, too modest and awkward to command much respect
or generate any fun. He seems to be losing his wife's affection, his
daughter's respect, and, by implication, control of his country's
future to his opposite number, a man with a surname that is familiar
to readers of nearly all Lurie's books – Zimmern.

Dan Zimmern is in theory a progressive, but in fact a Madison
Avenue materialist. Bill Hubbard is stingy, dull, unimaginative – and
responsible. Dan Zimmern is generous, lively, fanciful – and on the
prowl for sexual conquests, old and new. He is the father of Lennie,
14, who, like Erica Tate's children, is obnoxious. He will grow up to
be the formidably self-impressed critic, L. D. Zimmern, who in various ways darkens the lives of the women in the three novels that
follow *Only Children*. Dan is married to a pretty, neurotic, and conventional woman named Celia. She is protective of her daughter,
Lolly, and fearful of Lennie.

The fifth grown-up is Anna King, a self-appointed guardian of
traditional American values, an unmarried woman who cuts her own
wood. She has brought the families together, teaches the girls at her
progressive school Eastwind, and knew Dan Zimmern as a lover
many years before. She observes the games the other characters play
with the eyes of an old scout, looking for the strengths and flaws of
the contestants. Anna also has the novel's most probing soliloquy,
spoken in the presence of Honey, during which she explains what
has been her ballast at midlife, self-reliance. She builds a Frost-like
conceit out of the difficulty of finding one's way through dense forest
into open country, alone but not lonely. Honey mouths a weak case
for togetherness: "If there's people that need – Well, ah mean, when
somebody loves you – "

"I hate the word 'love,' " Anna responds. "It's like a kind of
nasty syrup people spread on things to disguise their real taste"
(243).

Anna's rejoinder has not gone unheard by Mary Ann. Eight pages
later, she adds her teacher's notions of love to those on sex and
babies she had formulated much earlier:

> Grown-ups and their magazines and newspapers talked about love as if it was
> a disease, like mumps and chicken pox, only it lasted longer. You didn't catch
> it from other people but from an invisible baby who shot arrows at you with
> germs of love on them, like the poisoned arrows of cannibal tribes. When one

of these arrows hit you the germs got into you and you had to be in love with
the next person you saw.
    Love made you sicker than chicken pox or even mumps. It was no wonder
Anna hated it as much as nasty medicine disguised with syrup. (251)

Lurie has programmed the entire book in this way. She juxta-
poses the tentative learning of the children, especially Mary Ann's,
with the syrupy strategies of their parents. She is especially skilled at
evoking the traumas that adult crimes and misdemeanors work on
youngsters. "When adults are children, children have to be adults,
and that is dreadful for them," writes Gordon (31).

"Grown-ups are supposed to act grown up," muses Mary Ann.
"But if they went on too long, it got sort of embarrassing and awful
and even scary." Listening to them can often be too much to take.
Mary Ann tunes out her mother whenever she says "honestly"
because it means she is lying, "like crossing your fingers behind your
back, only fairer . . . because anybody could notice it once they
caught on" (13). Her father loves his office near Times Square and
"is always . . . going back to it when he doesn't have to on Satur-
days." She and her father like organizing things into programs and
schedules, but Honey hates that. Mary Ann likes to make lists of all
the green leather things on her father's desk, which show how
important he is in his job of giving away money to poor people
during the Depression. ("The poor are always with us," her father
says to explain why he can always get a job even if the Republicans
take over.) She would like one brother and one sister, so she could
tell them what to do, but then she could have an awful brother, like
Lolly's (20).

Dreamy Lolly is far more impressionable than Mary Ann. She is
fair game for her half brother's vampire scares and imagines a
"Dracula wind" is blowing inside her. When Lennie proudly
announces that he has milked a cow, Lolly makes one of her characteristic imaginative leaps: she sees her mother and Mary Ann as
"cows, walking on their hands and feet in the grass, with pink naked
bulgy bags of milk hanging down [to be] grabbed and squeezed
twice a day by men's hands"(227-28). She vows never to be a cow
and thinks instead about smaller, less mind-boggling creatures,
especially mice. (Lolly's runaway imagination anticipates the misad-
venturous artist she grows up to be as the title character in Lurie's
The Truth about Lorin Jones.)

"No words are safe," says Lolly. "Nothing is safe and nobody. Everyone everywhere is vulgar horrible disgusting." One slides sideways through words: *ass*, for her, is one of those special Bible words that slide together wrong. Without warning, its holy sound slides into *behind*; your *behind* slides towards that most dangerous thing to talk about or, worse, let show: *panties*. She must never let any strange man or boy see her panties because even the good ones, like the handsome prince, can be changed into having to chase skirts, and no one can chase a skirt unless someone is wearing one. From her hidden window-seat refuge, Lolly has heard Bill Hubbard warning Honey of something she knows better than he: Dan Zimmern is a skirt-chaser (150-51).

Mary Gordon complains that occasionally Mary Ann and Lolly seem too old to have the thoughts they do. If I have an occasional problem with the girls, it is on opposite grounds. Both views are disingenuous. No novelist – no poet – can know in any naturalistic sense what really goes on in prepubescent consciousness. Everything becomes an accommodation. The children's insights must be true to the art of the literary work; no one, from the vantage of adulthood, can assess with certainty their trueness to life.

Gordon declares that in *Only Children*, where diction is so important, occasional lapses badly jar. It is, however, more important that lapses not occur in the reader's willingness to believe the ways these children expose the rules of the games grown-ups play. It is vital that the reader not only recognize the accuracy with which Lurie describes Mary Ann catching Japanese beetles in Anna's rosebushes but also accept that such a beetlehunt can take her underneath Anna's kitchen window, from which low vantage she, unseen, hears everything. What she hears is "mother talk," specifically, a devastating description of herself as "mah poor ugly duckling. Ah really can't imagine what's going to become of her" (159).

There ensues a passage, during which Mary Ann reflects on *ugly duckling*, that occupies about the same length as Lolly's on noisy, vulgar words. Lolly, however, has the safety of psychological distance. For Mary Ann, this *ugly duckling* is no noise from which she can flee. It has taken habitation within.

Mary Ann has no defense except a momentary reflection on the ugly duckling who grew up into a beautiful swan. But her mother did not describe Mary Ann in these terms; clearly Mary Ann has no hope for such a transformation. Rather, she has heard her mother extol marriage and bewail Mary Ann's chances ("She ought to have the option, you know what Ah mean?" [160]). Mary Ann defiantly releases the beetles ("Go on, eat up Anna's and everyone's flowers" [161]). She seeks comfort in her father but is turned away. She climbs on a chair to see herself in an antique mirror, and her reflection only confirms the accuracy of the word that now formulates her. *"What does it mean to be ugly"* (162)? Mary Ann's answer closes the novel. For the future, she will rule out love, live alone in a big house except for travel around the world, "and see every country there is and ride on camels and elephants and polar bears and hippopotamuses and kangaroos" (255). For the present, she will continue to dream of a dog named Woozle and a wish-box passport to living happily ever after.

As she recalls in "No One Asked Me to Write a Novel," Lurie knows firsthand what it's like to feel like an ugly duckling. *Only Children* marks her finest statement – from the inside – on childhood.

Children's Subversion: *Don't Tell the Grown-ups*

A scene from *Foreign Affairs* is a useful introduction to Lurie's disdain for overintellectualism and appreciation for the subversive in children's literature. A long-divorced American 54-year-old doyenne of folklore and children's literature undergoes an ordeal that calls into question the validity of her conception of herself. At the end of a long day's quest for rhymes that will at once add to her research in London and confirm a deep-seated Anglophilia and corresponding low regard for contemporary America, Vinnie Miner allows herself a rare indulgence in self-congratulation. But no sooner has she finished interviewing youngsters on a Camden Town playground than her assumptions about the superiority of English children to those she knows at home are shattered. A punkish urchin brazenly offers to share the sort of lyrics Vinnie may have missed – but for a price.

Mary Maloney's precocious shrewdness triumphs over Vinnie's instinctual snobbery. Mary's ditties feature four-letter words and ethnic disparagements, and they affront Vinnie's fragile defenses. After paying 50 pence a song, she declines "some really dirty ones," tries to shut off the child's taunts, and finally flees. As always, Vinnie opposes strategies of aggression with strategies of retreat. "Back in the sanctuary of her pleasant warm flat, with a pot of Twining's Queen Mary tea on the table before her next to the bowl of white hyacinths, Vinnie begins to feel better. She is able to pity Mary Maloney."[7]

Nonetheless, Vinnie has been jolted by the playground incident into an awareness of the provincial tidiness of her research. And she tries to shake it. She will forget Mary Maloney's rhymes, just as she has been habitually selecting out unpleasantries in adult folklore, comforting herself with the fact that she has included certain "off-color material":

> A scholar, of course, cannot afford to be prudish, and over the years she has recorded a good deal of off-color material with hardly a quiver. Children are given to bathroom humor:
>
>> Milk, milk, lemonade.
>> Around the corner fudge is made.
>
> She has even (without the accompanying gestures to parts of the body, of course) used this verse in her lectures as an example of folk metaphor, demonstrating the young child's undifferentiated pre-moral pleasure in both food and bodily products. (*Foreign Affairs*, 115-16)

Children and their literature are deserving of better than this, as Lurie argues in *Don't Tell the Grown-ups*.

Interviewed by Professor Dale Edmonds before an audience of English students at Tulane University in early 1986, Lurie extolled the "best" children's literature as "way up there" with the best adult writing and much more influential. Good children's books are for many Americans their only contact with first-rate writing. They shape our ideas, "tell us things about the world that go deeper often than the books we're going to read later, even if we go on reading serious literature."[8]

It is an article of faith with Lurie that the playful, imaginative, creative side of writing is a survival from the time when it was easy to invent and imagine the world in a magical way. In part, at least 12 of the 16 essays in *Don't Tell the Grown-ups* are dedicated to demonstrating that certain books stand as memorials of childhood.

Thus, in "The Boy Who Couldn't Grow Up," Lurie poignantly characterizes J. M. Barrie as an extreme case of the Peter Pan syndrome, marooned in childhood himself by a series of mordant deaths and attachments that in combination precluded inner growth. Thus, Edith Nesbit, who even more dramatically than Barrie, but to salutary effect, never quite grew up. She found it easy to speak in her books like one intelligent child to another in a way that shocked Victorian prudishness but which is today the usual mode of juvenile fiction. Thus Lurie has extracted from Arthur Mizener's biography of Ford Madox Ford evidence, not often drawn upon, for Ford's preference for fantasy over fact. Lost amidst a woefully uneven production of 81 books is *Christina's Fairy Book*. At the end of this book, says Lurie, Ford writes "with a pathos not entirely destroyed by self-pity" that his young daughters no longer call for him to read them fairy stories. They ask instead for "some history," thus disdaining the untruths that are most true and believing in the truths that are most false (*Grown-ups*, 90).

Although *New York Times* daily reviewer Michiko Kakutani is probably justified in charging that *Don't Tell the Grown-ups* reads less like a serious critical study of children's literature than a genial compilation of essays on some of Lurie's favorite authors, the reader has reason to be grateful for this.[9] Writing in the *New York Times Book Review*, Rosellen Brown finds the chapters focusing on a particular author make up the best sections of the book and gives special praise to the chapters on Victorian illustrator Kate Greenaway; myth-makers J. R. R. Tolkien and T. H. White, both viewed by Lurie as falling in the Kipling tradition of extolling the virtues of the British past, although from the respective vantages of medieval legend and the Arthurian chronicles; and, importantly, Frances Hodgson Burnet, on whose *Secret Garden* Rosellen Brown based a musical adaptation which has been performed in children's theaters.[10]

Lurie's interpretation of *The Secret Garden* may not be for everyone. It is, she writes, "the story of two unhappy, sickly, over-civilized children who achieve health and happiness through a combination of communal gardening, mystical faith, daily exercises, encounter-group-type confrontation, and a health-food diet" (*Grown-ups*, 144).

Some of her insights have been offered by others, as in her commentary on the fate of T. H. White, whose *Once and Future King* chronicles became *Camelot* on stage and in film, which in turn became a popular analogue for President John F. Kennedy's reign. Lurie writes that the Kennedy years had less in common with *Camelot* than with White's original chronicle, "with its flawed heroes, its inspiring public rhetoric and scandalous private revelations – and, of course, its awful end" (167).

Writing to a thesis is less in Alison Lurie's grain than capturing her readers with a series of little journeys into little-traveled territory. Such essays, published individually over a long span, are unlikely to be as powerful in the aggregate.

Subversion, especially in its alternate meaning of "overthrowing from the foundation," describes the main thrust of satire. The satirist jars long-assumed positions from their bases. Much great literature views life askant. For Lurie, the best writings in juvenile literature are like that. "They express ideas and emotions not generally approved of or even recognized at the time; they make fun of honored figures and piously held beliefs; and they view social pretenses with clear-eyed directness" (4).

What Alison Lurie wishes to subvert, through her essays in *Don't Tell the Grown-ups*, is the segregation of children and their literature from the larger life of the species.

In "The Folklore of Childhood," the final and most cogent essay in the collection, she demonstrates that all we need do is listen to them to know the ability of children to *belong*. If adults were to listen, the prevailing separatist illusion would be shattered. The notion that children can and should be protected from knowledge of the unpleasant would dissolve.

According to Jack K. Campbell, some childhood historians, notably Philippe Aries, point to earlier times when adults and children actually worked and played together. Without privacy, they experienced the same dangers and pleasures, shared the same secrets, the same world in all its raw brutality and wonderment. Together they partook of the same oral traditions and stories, whether sacred or profane. Eventually, the idea of childhood as we know it was invented. The life of the child became sequestered, protected from the adult world. Children were exiled into a world of their own.[11] In the seventeenth century, at about the same time that children began to be viewed as creatures with special needs and not as merely small adults, a separate literature for children appeared. Like childhood itself, children's literature became exiled from adult literature.

In his *Centuries of Childhood*, Aries views parent-child relations as in steady deterioration. The indifference paid to the child before the seventeenth century was replaced not with more help and consideration but with more severity, couched in an "obsessive love" that deprived the child of the freedom he had hitherto enjoyed among adults.[12]

It is beyond the scope of this book to confront the implications of the systematic removal of the child from adult society and the concomitant partitioning of children's literature. Lurie's "The Folklore of Childhood" presents a variety of proofs that document what *Only Children* dramatizes – that while the grown-ups have lost touch with the children, the children have never lost touch with us.

Chapter Six

Foreign Affairs

James again, Fred thinks: [*the real thing* is] a Jamesian phrase, a Jamesian situation. But in the novels the scandals and secrets of high life are portrayed as more elegant; the people are better mannered. Maybe because it was a century earlier; or maybe only because the mannered elegance of James's prose obfuscates the crude subtext. Maybe, in fact, it was just like now.

– Alison Lurie, *Foreign Affairs*

Lessons of the Master: A Jamesian Reading

The ghost of Henry James and of his own favorite of his novels, *The Ambassadors* (1903), hovers over *Foreign Affairs* (1984), Alison Lurie's Pulitzer Prize-winning and seventh novel. I am not suggesting that she deliberately set out to write a modern novel in the mode of James. I do claim, however, that Lurie has *superintended* this book in a manner that is peculiarly Jamesian. It is both James the supreme aesthetician of the novel and James the supreme celibate concerned about his unlived life who looms above every development in *Foreign Affairs.*

The quest in *Foreign Affairs* is for the authentic self, largely embodied in the inner life of its heroine, a 54-year-old teacher-scholar of children's literature. Through an affair with a brash yet loving married American, Vinnie Miner temporarily reverses what has been the central paradox of her life: a desire to have experience without involvement. Chuck Mumpson initially represents everything Vinnie abhors, but curiosity can temper reticence when a worthier sensibility is touched. These are also central Jamesian themes. They are the major concerns of *The Ambassadors.*

The Ambassadors and *Foreign Affairs* are both chronicles of awakenings and reconciliations. James's "ambassador," Lambert Strether, is a middle-aged New Englander who is dispatched by his

American patron to bring home her son, Chad Newsome, who has lingered too long in Paris. As Leon Edel observes, James shows Strether, a man "strapped tight by his New England 'conditioning,' unwind in the Parisian circle"[1] of Chad Newsome, the object of his mission, and come to an eleventh-hour realization that changes his life: one "lives" by one's receptivity to experience. He and his sponsors at home have closed all their doors to life.

Strether's awakening is hard earned. So taken is he by Chad's friends – especially Madame de Vionnet, an aristocratic French lady with a grown daughter, and a young artist named John Little Bilham – that he despairs of his empty life. He defies his sponsors in refusing to carry out his mission to bring Chad home, but he also resists the truth; namely, that Chad's Parisian education has included taking Madame de Vionnet as his mistress. The book's climactic scene makes Strether privy to Chad's liaison with the very person who had sparked his rebirth. Awaiting dinner at an inn near a river, Strether sees a boat containing the informally dressed lovers.

This scene at the close of the book combines with an equally famous one from the beginning of Strether's embassy to define James's statement. In the earlier scene, Strether urges Little Bilham, the American expatriate-artist, to "live." "Live all you can; it's a mistake not to. It doesn't so much matter what you do in particular so long as you have your life." He goes on: "One has the illusion of freedom; therefore don't be, like me, without the memory of that illusion."[2] Strether is given the illusions of freedom by Paris. Even though he returns to New England, he will no longer measure life by the narrow standards of the New World.

Vinnie Miner, like Strether, is an American on an embassy abroad. If fewer Americans today are sent by patrons on "rescue" missions to the fleshpots of Europe than were sent a century ago, more by far travel there on sabbaticals. Such are Vinnie and a 29-year-old fellow academic named Fred Turner. Both teach at Corinth University.

The plot of *Foreign Affairs*, like that of *The Ambassadors*, is about that comedy of manners which Kingsley Amis calls "being abroad." Vinnie is "small, plain, and unmarried – the sort of person no one ever notices, though she is an Ivy League professor [with] a well-established reputation in the expanding field of children's literature" (*Foreign Affairs*, 1). Fred, a young scholar of eighteenth-century English literature, matinee-idol handsome, is, unhappily, on the verge of divorcing his wife. He is in London to retrace the foot-steps of the satirical Restoration poet John Gay (1685-1732), whose early burlesque, *Trivia; or, The Art of Walking the Streets of London* (1716), well describes Fred Turner's activities. Fred finds himself in situations he persistently sees as Jamesian.

After succumbing to a destructive infatuation for Rosemary Radley, a popular British television star who aspires to play Lady Macbeth, Fred finds himself a weekend guest of an English profes-sional hostess named Posy Billings. Posy has arranged for three sets of lovers, including a male pair, to be united at her Victorian country house. A suggestively costumed erotic version of charades is about to start when Posy's husband, believed to be in Ankara, arrives. A comic scene ensues as Fred becomes entangled in the efforts to rid the house of any evidence of Posy's lover, William. Despite his strong temptation to flee this Henry James scene of old-world wickedness, he instead exercises a kind of William Jamesian pragmatism and helps Posy.

Not yet aware of her true nature, Fred sees Rosemary as "the classic James heroine: beautiful, fine, delicate, fatally impul-sive . . . too generous to see [her friends] as they are, too light-hearted and trusting." He believes he must rescue her from "two posturing queers and a bossy adulteress whose hair looks like a wig – though only an hour ago he thought it was all beautiful, *the real thing*" (107).

For a time, Fred follows Strether's example and forgets his spon-sors back home, including his wife. He indulges his sense of having got into a James novel, finding it both numbing and exhilarating.

As for Vinnie, she has never envisioned her life as other than a series of tableaux out of Jane Austen. *Foreign Affairs* presents her with the illusion, unexpectedly, that she can for once play life's games by different rules from those she has learned from literary models. For some of Vinnie's key scenes, Lurie creates an imaginary dog named Fido, who appears whenever she is giving in to self-pity.

Vinnie knows London. She has a circle of friends and a defensive snobbery. When, on the plane to London, she at first avoids an Oklahoma engineer named Chuck Mumpson, she is assailed as directly as Strether, under the charms of Madame de Vionnet, by the poverty of the human relations in her life. It is only, as Lorna Sage observes in her review of *Foreign Affairs,* "when Fido leaves her, and she imagines him trailing Chuck instead, that we know she has broken the rules that make minor characters out of people like herself."[3] For Vinnie

> English literature . . . has suddenly fallen silent. Now, at last, all those books have no instructions for her, no demands – because she is just too old.
> In the world of classic British fiction, the one Vinnie knows best, almost the entire population is under fifty. . . . People over fifty who aren't relatives are pushed into minor parts, character parts, and are usually portrayed as comic. . . . The literary convention is that nothing can happen to them. (*Foreign Affairs,* 206)

Vinnie's counsel to herself follows her type-casting and flies in the face of Strether's advice to Little Bilham. In another passage, a heightened parody of romance fiction as reconstructed by a worldly matron who has read much, Lurie writes:

> Vinnie tells herself again that it is time, and past time, to leave what her mother used to refer to as All That behind. It is time to steer past the Scylla and Charybdis of elderly sexual farce and sexual tragedy into the wide, calm sunset sea of abstinence, where the tepid waters are never troubled by the burning heat and chill, the foamy backwash and weed-choked turbulence of passion. (81)

As the over-protesting quality of the passage foreshadows, Vinnie is certain to succumb to the sanitary engineer from Tulsa – a giving lover, the reverse of her accustomed lot.

> "Wait," Vinnie tries to say between kisses, in which somehow she has begun to join. "I'm not sure I want. . . . " But her voice now entirely refuses to function; and her body – rebellious, greedy, – presses itself against Chuck's. Now, it cries: more, more. Very well, she says to it. Very well, if you insist. Just this once. After all, no one will ever have to know. (183)

Lurie makes sure the reader knows. Here and throughout the novel Lurie uses a narrative voice as a sort of selective palimpsest, an overlay on the action. This voice observes the seriocomic play of manners wholly in present tense in order the better to signal the reader to recognizable "home" situations against which Lurie's two Americans abroad appear to be rebelling. The narrator focuses on

Vinnie and Fred in turns, as the unfolding of comic manners requires.

Lurie and James: "Exhibitional Conditions to Meet"

It is in her concern not to violate the fidelity of point of view that Alison Lurie is especially Jamesian. Although neither he nor any novelist in English until the modern era wrote novels in the present tense (Laurence Sterne, in *Tristram Shandy*, being a conditional exception), Henry James would surely have been struck by Lurie's version of his own narrative strategies. She posts above Vinnie Miner and Fred Turner a monitoring consciousness that is seasoned, wise, and above temporary enchantments. James referred to his system of narrative focus as the Central Intelligence. It is the solidly posed center that resides wholly in Strether. James was 60 when he most fully made the consciousness of the onlooker the central focus of a major novel.

Entering his final phase at the turn of the century, James was wrestling with the compromise fiction exacts from life. Rebecca West's axiom expresses that compromise as well as it can be done: "There is no conversation; there are intersecting monologues."[4] The serious reader shares the same awareness as the serious novelist. Having in most matters but a single point of view, and listening to someone, we hear what is said from our own angle. Or, speaking ourselves, we know why we say what we do, but may only guess at what is going on in our listener's mind.

James made an ideal of holding his story so firmly in its frame that he could, like a prestidigitator, fully control what is *seen*. For James, *control* was vital. For Alison Lurie, three-quarters of a century later, control is the cornerstone of her fictive art. *The Ambassadors*, writes James in his preface, "has exhibitional conditions to meet."[5] He means that he has an obligation to *show*, not merely *tell*, what is motivating Strether. So does Lurie. She meets them through a variation on the central intelligence.

Like Strether, Vinnie is apprehensive from the start. As she settles into her airline berth to begin her lightly funded research sabbatical, she turns over in her mind the possibilities latent in her chance encounter with wealthy retired engineer Chuck Mumpson. Lurie reverts to the historical past tense when she allows Vinnie to review a failed marriage that has been followed by a series of real and fantasy adventures and misadventures.

> Vinnie always ended her real affairs whenever she found her current lover getting into her bedtime home movies, or when one of them began to use the word "love" casually, or to announce that he could really imagine getting seriously involved with her. No thanks, chum; I was caught that way once before, she would think to herself. Not that there was always a current lover. For long periods Vinnie's only companions were the shades of Richard Wilbur, Robert Penn Warren, etc., who faithfully every evening appeared to admire and embrace her, commending her wit, charm, intelligence, scholarly achievement, and sexual inventiveness. (80)

Sabbaticals should leave their recipients refreshed. If recognizing anew the satisfactions of the familiar can renew as well as refresh, Vinnie and Fred have made gains. Vinnie's choice is made especially easy; Lurie has Chuck Mumpson die of a heart attack. Vinnie muses, but not too sadly, over the possibility that she and Chuck might have gone on being Londoners had Chuck lived; that she might have quit her job at Corinth and given all her time to research and writing. Her self-assessment is cut from the Jamesian mold of self-denial. How stupid of someone like her to go on like this: "It's not what she wants at all, not what would ever have worked, even if Chuck were alive. It's not her nature, not her fate to be loved, to live with anyone; her fate is to be always single, unloved, alone" (290).

Just as at the beginning, Lurie takes still another tip from James. The imaginary dog, Fido, introduced as an invisible companion en route to London, is at her heels at the conclusion of the novel. Fido, in effect, has been a "*ficelle*"; that is, as James borrowed the word from the French, an accessory character used to convey both information and vital signals without having to resort to "the *terrible* fluidity of self-revelation."

Lurie sends Fred back to America, his academic mission unfulfilled, but perhaps domestically restored to his wife, Roo, who, like her father, the self-impressed critic L. D. Zimmern, has made earlier appearances in Lurie's fiction.

Chapter Seven

The Language of Clothes

Fictive Signs and Signals

In Alison Lurie's fiction appearances frequently deceive, but they do not go unmarked. In *Love and Friendship*, Brian Holman falls in love with Emily at first sight. As is frequently the case in Lurie's novels, a character is attracted to something that contrasts pleasantly with what has jaded him.

> The childish, clumsy, innocent look had attracted him; sitting exactly in the center of a brocaded chair, she was like one of those good, plump, well-cared-for little girls who are photographed for *Vogue* in velvet dresses with white collars and white gloves, ready for dancing school. He was so damned tired of all the girls he had known: the overdressed semivierges [*sic*] at college who had seen everything at eighteen. . . . Emmy's obvious inexperience, even ignorance, of the ways of the world was all to the good. She was intelligent, ready to learn, and he could form her mind. In these matters, like many men, he preferred the damp clay to the Ming vase. (*L&F*, 231)

Brian will learn, as Lurie's husbands often do, that the domestic blend he has catalog-ordered to his tastes will change if heady new elements are introduced.

Katherine Cattleman in *The Nowhere City* has never been to a beach party–Southern California style. She has found a good job and a good lover. Now she must do something about her appearance. Iz, her boss and lover, suggests she try the stores in Beverly Hills. As she walks toward Beverly Boulevard, all the shoppers seem costumed for a chorus line or a comic book. Where were the summer suits everyone wore in Boston or New York? "Look at the women. . . . They wore high-heeled sandals, tight pants in metallic colors or fluorescent pastels, and brief tops which often left a strip of bare skin around the waist" (*Nowhere City*, 237). A 20-foot wide graphic in cardboard depicts a life-sized woman climbing to the brim of a cup of coffee. The message reverberates in her consciousness: "Indulge Yourself."

Brian (*The War between the Tates*) initially responds to Wendy Gahaghan because of her supreme ordinariness, which contrasts with his memories of his wife, Erica, at Radcliffe: honor student, elegantly dressed, extraordinarily pretty. Wendy dresses in Indian style, but – like his kids – confuses Eastern and Western varieties.

> She wore, indiscriminately, paisley-bedspread shifts, embroidered velvet slippers, fringed cowhide vests and moccasins, strings of temple bells, saris, shell beads, sandals, and leather pants very loose in the ankle and tight in the ass. In spite of all this paraphernalia, she never looked like either sort of Indian. Rather, she resembled a solemn schoolchild. (*The Tates*, 38)

Eight months later, having moved out of Erica's and into Wendy's, Brian determines his mistress "ought to wear rose, creamy white, lavender . . . ; also her clothes should fit, rather than hang. Something might be done about her hair, too" (210).

When Vinnie Miner, hopeful of acculturating her Americanness within the swank of Fortnum and Mason's, encounters the Tulsa engineer for a second time, the clashes in his Western getup loom as an affront: "Chuck Mumpson peels off his plastic raincoat, revealing a brown Western-cut leather jacket trimmed with leather fringe, a shiny-looking yellow Western-cut shirt with pearlized studs instead of buttons, and a leather string tie" (*Foreign Affairs*, 71). But clothes make the man. In Lurie's fiction clothing helps create character. They tell the truth, too, as Janet of *Real People* recognizes when, her thinking triggered by the adjectives in the dust-jacket blurb for her first book, she is "reminded of the 'certain kind of woman' in the Peck & Peck ads, who has such charming, feminine, witty, etc., tastes, but always dresses with dowdy conventionality. One knows that her clothes tell the real truth, and her advertised enthusiasm for dandelions and French poetry is sheer affectation" (*Real People*, 58).

What the above selections from five of Alison Lurie's novels share is that each sends out an unspoken signal from one character to another – or to self – through the language of clothes. The value of clothing in Lurie's fiction is socially derived. Vinnie must jump over the shadow of class and cultural bias, as represented by Chuck's rustic accoutrements, to locate the value within. The elegant Rosemary Radley, dressed always to deceive, will find her authenticity in living the role of a brassy charwoman.

The Language of Clothes

During the winter of 1980, Alison Lurie told her friend David Jackson that she was doing her first nonfiction book, which would ultimately be published as *The Language of Clothes* (1981). Its subject should not have been surprising to her readers.

> The idea [she explained to Jackson] is the language of clothes; it will explain to you what your clothes mean. It's based on the premise that we are speaking to each other continually through what we wear and how our hair is done. When people meet each other at a party, or on the street, before they even speak they are saying something to each other through their clothes. As many people have pointed out before, clothing is a language.[1]

Clothes, she went on, have the same potential for self-expression as language. To Jackson's objection that a woman ought not to be held to dressing authentically when she barges into a shop and grabs something off the rack, Lurie responded that what the rush shopper is really saying is, "Don't hold me too accountable for what my clothes are saying . . . " (Jackson, 21).

Lurie acknowledges what some critics would charge; namely, that the correlation between clothes and language can never be exact. What really links words and clothing for her as a novelist is intonation. The *way* something is worn may be more important than the item itself.

One often reads, most commonly in explications of poems, that *what* the words mean is less important than *how* they mean. It is the same with a style – whether of clothing or of a prose passage – that seeks an effect. In the heightened parody of romance fiction quoted from *Foreign Affairs* in chapter 5 ("It is time to steer past the Scylla and Charybdis of elderly sexual farce," etc.), Lurie deliberately overwrites to convey the impression of a woman who has for so long been living by the books that she has contrived her denial of living in terms that are as true to art as they are false to life.

Lurie evokes the *how* of dress in the novel's Rosemary Radley, demonstrating that her manner of wearing anything from a gauzy blouse to a hairstyle provides the key to her character, at least as viewed by Vinnie.

> Everything she wears shimmers and billows and dangles; she seems not so much dressed as loosely draped in flimsy, flowery, lacy stuffs: veils and scarves and floating gauzy blouses and trailing skirts and fringed silk shawls. Her hair is continually in flux: tinted and streaked in varying shades from pale gold to bisque, it alternately gathers itself up in soft coils, falls in flossy clouds about her shoulders, or extends wayward tendrils and curls in all directions. (*Foreign Affairs*, 119-20)

In passages such as this Lurie illustrates fictionally what her social history of apparel documents. She concludes: "We can lie in the language of dress, or try to tell the truth; but unless we are naked and bald it is impossible to be silent."[2]

In *The Language of Clothes*, Lurie gives voice to what we wear. She maintains that a vigilant clothes watcher can locate a complete grammar, a syntax capable of being diagrammed, a lexicon that usage has standardized in the way an updated dictionary standardizes language. But for all its sweep, the best things in the book are products of the novelist's cataloguing eye.

The reader learns minutiae on a wide array of topics. The frogged fastenings that once adorned military uniforms were derived from the bare ribs of the skeletons that soldiers had painted on themselves to frighten the enemy. If it is true that one of the desirable accompaniments to aging is to be able to recover degrees of innocence, one warms to Lurie's correct observation that the sports clothes of the adult are the everyday clothes of the child. Lurie conjectures that the unusual length of christening gowns was originally a way of wishing long life for the baby in an age of high infant mortality.

It should not come as a surprise that *Foreign Affairs* immediately followed *The Language of Clothes*. Among the details the reader retains long after finishing the novel are the selective ones about Chuck Mumpson – the furled umbrella, the green plastic raincoat, the pair of scuffed loafers – that signify the Oklahoman's engaging diffidence, which will bring down Vinnie Miner from her lofty provinciality.

The Language of Clothes, as a compendium of clothing as metaphor, suffered in a small way the fate among specialists that H. G. Wells's *Outline of History* had experienced 60 years before.[3] Such critics usually praised Lurie's novelistic skills in popularizing and lightening the weight of documentation. ("The book may never be used as a standard text," writes J. D. Reed in *Time,* "but it is ideal for those who want to slip into something more comfortable."[4]) But some found her efforts at more serious analysis less rewarding.

Political writer Walter Goodman, for example, finds a tendency to overreach. He questions Lurie's connection of popular Western garb to the right-wing shift in America's politics. "That sounds right only to the extent that Ronald Reagan and Larry Hagman happen to look so natural in boots and 10-gallon hat that they are being copied, as celebrities often are."[5]

Anne Hollander, author of the much-respected *Seeing through Clothes* (1978), differs sharply with Lurie on mid-nineteenth-century female dress. She is critical of Lurie's descriptions of the many-layered costume worn by Victorian women. "Although she was so heavily armored against a frontal assault," Lurie notes, the mid-Victorian woman was often readily accessible in another direction, since she had no underpants" (*Clothes,* 219). Hollander replies:

> Lurie has fallen for the idea that all mid-nineteenth-century female dress was something awful called "Victorian," of which the very forms embodied an ideal of weak-minded and hopelessly immobilized femininity, and of which the single right opinion is that we are well out of it. She fails to remember that the many-skirted, deep-bonneted, tight-corseted mode was invented in Paris and worn with great panache by the free-living *"lorettes"* and *"lionnes"* of French Romantic bohemianism, as well as by the strong-willed *grandes cocottes* and sagacious *grandes bourgeoises* and *petites midinettes* who figure so vividly in French fiction and art. The complex trappings of the nineteenth-century female had their aggressive as well as their passive aspects; like modern high heels, they could be enabling as well as inhibiting.[6]

Hollander finds the book's underlying theme simplistic. By emphasizing the inability of dress to "shut up," Lurie undermines its language as worthwhile. As she describes it, Hollander argues, the language of clothes is speech with no literature; basically a primitive yawp, intrusive, from which little substantive communication can issue.

Hollander's review provides a liberal education in distinguishing between art and life in the matter of dress. "When Alison Lurie says, 'The woman in the sensible gray wool suit and frilly pink blouse is a serious, hard-working mouse with a frivolous and feminine soul,' she is not being realistic but novelistic – or possibly theatrical." Her main criticism comes down to Lurie's being a novelist rather than a professional in the signification of clothing. "Discussing clothes as if they were costumes for characters has only the rough validity proper to a morality play or a soap opera. In life, there is usually more to it, or often much less. . . . A high-necked blouse may be worn because of some bargain one is striking with the persuasive suggestions of commercial art, not because of one's need to express modesty" (Hollander, 38).

Even so, for the student of literature, *The Language of Clothes* is a treasure of allusion. In fact, it is by such references that Lurie charts historical change. Shakespeare, Goethe, Fielding, Austen, Dickens, Eliot, Trollope, James, Wilde, Conrad, Colette, and F. Scott Fitzgerald are cited to show how the contemporary reader, familiar with prevailing styles, could deduce from the appearance of characters their age, class, origins, opinions and mood.

Lurie's talents as a storyteller also distinguish the book from others on the topic. She delves into various closets to discover an array of contrasts. The career woman who totes an attaché case and a quilted handbag is sending out clashing signals. The nouveau riche film wunderkind who wears an $800 sports coat over a J. C. Penney denim shirt is flaunting his wealth while pretending to disregard it.

While Lurie should not be classed as a regional writer, her novels are rich in local color. Clothes articulate the variances in regional costume that invalidate any idea that, considering commercial mass production and distribution, Americans tend to look alike. Reed explains: "At home, what [Lurie] deems 'regional speech' controls fashion. New Englanders still favor the conservative and tweedy British look. The white dress embellished with large flowers reigns in the South as an announcement that one can afford a laundress. Midwestern men favor suits the color of plowed cornfields. The Western states bloom with cowboy boots and ten-gallon hats (Reed, 96). Lurie reserves her vitriol for the "California style." "Virtuous working-class housewives may wear outfits that in any other part of the country would identify them as medium-priced whores," she writes (*Clothes*, 113).

The Language of Clothes, for all the wide-ranging excavations into the literature of fashion and clothing, is essentially a byproduct of the novelist's art. Lurie writes that "the most striking thing about British dress, both urban and rural, is its tendency to follow the principle of camouflage" (*Clothes*, 102). Theatrical county clothes contrive to hint at rural associations without being suited to rural life. Camouflage, or disguise, lives a life of its own in *Foreign Affairs*. Vinnie Miner's disguises aim to belie her fears, as expressed on the opening page, that at 54 she is "the sort of person that no one ever notices." It is age she seeks to camouflage once she settles in London.

Occasionally life reveals the full price of disguise when it is adopted to satisfy an insatiable public. Actor George Reeves ended his life in 1959 because he was unable to accept the world's estimate of him as Superman.[7] One of literature's finest capabilities is that of probing beneath the disguises life exacts – among them, protectives such as clothing – to touch feelings that resist detection.

Chapter Eight

Imaginary Friends

Alison Lurie, in a composite review of John Updike's novel *S.* and his short-story collection *Trust Me*, implicitly endorses Graham Greene's description of some of his own early novels as "entertainments" rather than novels. If Updike "had called his minor works 'entertainments,' *jeux d'esprit* such as *The Coup* and *The Witches of Eastwick* might have met with less resistance."[1] Likewise, *Imaginary Friends* (1967), though not a minor work, could be called an entertainment.

Lurie may have had an entirely different audience in mind for her third novel than for her first two. While *Love and Friendship* and *The Nowhere City* are about marriage and adultery in academic settings, *Imaginary Friends* has the atmosphere of science fiction. The cover for the Avon paperback edition bears all the ingredients: a golden-robed medium appears to have conjured up a naked creature suggestive of a martian, whose pointed ears recall Mr. Spock of *Star Trek*. The medium on the cover is a "mad" teenage dropout named Verena, leader of a sect called the Truth Seekers. The other worldly creature is Ro of the planet Varna. The image of Ro is purely the artist's conception; he is never actually seen by anyone in the novel. It is the purported words of Ro, as translated extrasensorily by Verena, that give the novel the feeling of science fiction

The setting of *Imaginary Friends*, however, is in many respects traditional. The action takes place in a rural upstate New York village, significantly named Sophis, suggestive of the sophistry that characterizes the behavior of nearly everyone in the book. Sophists indeed are the small-town faddists, the Truth-Seekers, who look to Ro's words for easy answers, as are the two university sociologists who have wormed their way into the Seekers' seances for a field study.

Lurie refrains from an obviously satirical delivery. She is as nondirective in narrative stance as Roger Zimmern,[2] the novel's young central intelligence, believes he is in his research methods. Zimmern and his senior partner, Thomas McManus, formerly a controversial wunderkind, more lately a tarnished opportunist, want to understand the nature of group conflict. Lurie leaves hardly a folkway of the 1960s unscathed, from reliance on the "right vibes" to food faddism.

During her former husband's doctoral studies at Harvard, Lurie worked as an assistant to sociologists. The experience spurred a critical interest in the social sciences as well as in psychology, astrology, and witchcraft. Judging from *Imaginary Friends*, she has practiced what applied sociology preaches – that is, that most phenomena, material or nonmaterial, can be explained by the right surveys. Now Lurie not only wishes to refute that position but to indicate its human toll on all concerned. Her larger aim appears to be to confront "science" and "superstition" to disturb complacency.

What I have loosely called a conflict between science and superstition, British critic Judie Newman refers to as a contrast between "two forms of truth-seeking, the objective and rational . . . and the mystical and committed."[3] For Newman, whose readings of this hybrid fiction are by far the most dialectically "packed" to date,

> the novel draws upon the ethical ambiguities of sociological strategies, in order to make both literary and political points. When Tom McMann and Roger Zimmern set up a small-group interaction study of the Seekers, they use classic methods: participant observation, role play, and non-directive techniques. As a result, in their search for truth they begin by adopting false identities and lying comprehensively to the Seekers. (Newman, 7)

Of course, no novel of ideas can succeed as dramatic fiction unless the ideas are galvanized dramatically. *Imaginary Friends* must be "peopled," too, and it is. As long as Roger, as a participant observer, believes he can observe the Seekers without emotional involvement, the novel seems bloodless. Once Roger satisfies the reader that he doesn't care about hanging onto McManus's sociological coattails or seeing the Truth Seekers as anything more than born-again, bigoted provincials, *Imaginary Friends* takes flight. When he reveals himself to be physically attracted to Verena, although still wary of her, the novel begins to elicit the psychic investment of the reader. "The only thing in Sophis that still interested me was Verena. I was convinced that she had some sort of ability, some special sensitivity, that most people anywhere lacked. This ability had nothing to do with the superstructure of dogma that had been imposed on it."[4]

Verena's special sensitivity notwithstanding, Lurie presents her followers as fatuous ideologues. At one point, a schism threatens Verena's rules, causing, as Newman notes, "a sharp shift from an original Transcendental cast toward a more Manichean, sin-oriented creed" (Newman, 7). Lurie writes:

> Previously . . . [the] universe was full of benevolent power; Spiritual Light and Cosmic Love were flowing more and more towards Sophis, New York. Ro's messages and Verena's advice [had been] filled with joyful reassurance. . . . Now a more Manichean tone, a kind of metaphysical shadow, began to spread. . . . There were terrible weaknesses within our spirits, we had to realize, and menacing forces without. We heard much more about the elementals now. They were no longer just a kind of spiritual bad weather . . . ; they were sentient forces, full of contagious, stupid malevolence. (*Imaginary Friends*, 109)

Writing in *Commonweal*, Irving Malin stresses Lurie's deft balancing of the deadpan and the mysterious.[5] Combining them, she presents the Seekers' unquestioning conformity to Ro's Verena-relayed catalog of prohibitions. The Seekers are allowed a diet suitable to a tame rabbit. Its exclusions mock the macrobiotic food crazes of the 1960s and the health food diets that remain popular. "Light-colored foods were preferable to dark ones, and a low specific gravity was good. . . . dairy products (milk, butter, cheese) had strong life vibrations. . . . Eggs were questionable; while steak, chicken, ham, and fish were full of heavy, decaying electricity: not only were they dead, they were murdered" (133).

Lurie's Seekers represent the range of gullibility she finds in American society generally. Zimmern realizes that his acceptance of McMann's opportunism makes him worse than the Seekers, whose Ro is simply another name for God and whose rituals are merely provincial Protestantism. He has allowed himself to be a knowing accomplice. An inner voice whispers the only truth he has allowed himself to hear since arriving among the Sophists: "You become the role you play" (*Imaginary Friends*, 234).

Role playing, in fact, dominates the final fourth of the book. In a weak parody of Christian myth, Verena relates Ro of Varna's promise of a Coming. The Truth Seekers gather in the freezing upstate winter to await final revelation in their leader's Aunt Emily's backyard. Well past midnight, after eight hours of invocations and off-key singing reminiscent of an evangelical cult, Verena hushes her disciples, points to a corner of the backyard and a glow in the sky. A shivering Zimmern recognizes the reflection of the lights of downtown Sophis on low-hanging clouds.

Verena collapses in the snow and mud and, with her, the promise of Coming collapses as well. Aunt Emily is quick to recognize that without a medium such as Verena the Seekers will disperse. She announces that Ro has chosen to enter their sphere, but through a single spirit – that of Tom McMann.

Given this turn of events, the only way Lurie can resolve the loose ends of the plot and keep the atmosphere of pseudoscience and superstition alive is by a series of ambiguities. McMann either accepts Verena's mantle in order to continue his research or he really believes he has been transmogrified into being Ro of Varna; Lurie does not make clear which is the case. She allows Zimmern to take a position that is akin to that of someone like R. D. Laing: the mad offer more than the so-called well. "All madness after all (I thought) is just exaggeration of some norm. Respect becomes reverence; the group leader becomes a prophet or a god. . . . Among the Seekers, he could be worshipped again as the bringer of Truths of Light, but under another name" (266).

Four months after the flawed Coming and its violent aftermath which have led to McMann's arrest and comfortable confinement to a rural state hospital, Zimmern makes a last visit to the senior sociologist. Already McMann is making a survey – from inside – of the mental patients, a further study of small-group dynamics. His longer-range plans call for continuance as Ro of Varna, but with a growing constituency.

With a threatening gesture, Tom dismisses Roger as a fool and a coward. And so he has been. But to the extent that Roger now wonders if he should remain in a field that is so bereft of humanity, he has grown. "Apparently, in spite of all those books and articles on roleplaying, we consider ourselves immune from our own laws. We think we're exempt from ordinary moral laws too: when we mess around with people's lives, either we aren't really doing it, or it somehow doesn't count" (285-86).

Far more than an entertainment, *Imaginary Friends* is "dialectical but in every way more ambitious" than the two novels preceding it, according to Newman. She acknowledges Lurie's ambiguity about whether Verena wrote the messages consciously or not. But Newman finds the book's ambiguity "productive." For her, Lurie, above all, leaves open the possibility that Tom and others like him will lead the Seekers "into a mass movement . . . first as a mass delusion, and then as a respectable religious movement. Like *One Flew over the Cuckoo's Nest, Catch-22,* and *The Crying of Lot 49,* the novel takes as its theme the absence of any obvious distinction between sane and insane in a society in which the norm is consensually defined by the majority" (Newman, 8). Indeed, one is prompted to see in Tom McMann a fictional anticipation of Jim Jones and his People's Temple.

Although sexual intrigue provides the touchstone for all but one of her first five novels, that one, *Imaginary Friends,* consolidates her talent as a satirist who eschews hyperbole while combining fantasy and actuality.

Chapter Nine

Alison Lurie and the Critics

The Media's Massage

Reviewers, by and large, have treated Alison Lurie well but superficially, as a sampling of dust-jacket endorsements reflects: poet James Merrill called her "the wisest woman in America"; Truman Capote believed *The War between the Tates* was a book Jane Austen would enjoy; Gore Vidal crowned her the "Queen Herod of modern fiction." *The War between the Tates* brought her a place on the bestseller list, an international audience, and a media image as an irreverent satirist of middle-brow America.

Fortunately for sales but unfortunately for Lurie's credibility as a serious novelist, she has for nearly two decades been locked into this image. John Skow set the tone with his flippantly respectful review in *Time* of *The War between the Tates* ("In this summerweight comedy of hanky-panky in a university town, the apple is a little mushy, but worm and novel are in the best of health").[1] The three columns of text framed a photograph of Lurie, looking at once coy and wicked from beneath a wide-brimmed hat. Ten years later she was a tenured full professor at Cornell, and *Newsweek*, in a review of *Foreign Affairs*, accentuated her academic persona with an apparently unposed classroom snapshot. But Lurie's "reputation for mordant wit and coldblooded satire," as David Lehman puts it, remained intact. "I don't think I'm as cruel as I'm made out to be," Lurie says. "*Foreign Affairs* is my seventh novel, and it's the first time I've ever killed off a single character. The people in my books may be ridiculed, but they don't lose their jobs, get run over by trucks or succumb to fatal diseases. The worse that can happen to them is that some of their illusions are exposed."[2]

The War between the Tates: "An Annoying Book"

Reviews in the academic and intellectual press often praise Lurie's virtues before shooting her down for the perceived defects of these virtues. The most searching of this type of critique may have been John Leonard's essay on *The War between the Tates* in *New Republic.* After likening her to a surgeon putting on gloves before sitting down at her typewriter, Leonard summarizes the plot with skill and economy. He heralds the style ("faultless prose, like an English lawn [where] one could play polo"), ticks off a half-dozen "brilliant scenes," and appears to marvel at the novelist's "detachment so profound that we might be looking at tropical fish in a tank instead of people in extremis."[3] He then confesses to having found *The War between the Tates* an "annoying book." He charges Lurie with "punishing the Tates" for their anachronistic noblesse oblige, which leaves them at the end, in Erica's words, "ugly, foolish, guilty, and dying." He deplores the programmatic analogies between war and what goes on between wives and husbands who are unhappy with each other. "The metaphor weighs a ton. Containment, escalation, guerilla warfare, hostages, are not so much alluded to as forced down the reader's throat. . . . [and] our foreign policy is not an extension of our boredom in the bedroom or our loathing of teenaged ingrates or our self-righteousness about marriage vows" (Leonard, 25).

Leonard makes his points well, but he overlooks Lurie's prerogative to put her characters through a punishing process that may be necessary if they are to move, even tentatively, toward self-knowledge. Leonard concludes by attacking Lurie's coldness, even contempt, in the face of human travail. John Cheever and John Updike have also walked on Lurie's "turf," Leonard says, "Updike seeking some lyrical equivalent of the joy of discovery and the pain of betrayal" and Cheever finding "a redeeming humanity, sorrow instead of disgust." In *The War between the Tates,* however, "Alison Lurie refuses to sympathize, and so this marvelously polished, splendidly crafted novel creates an antiseptic space in the mind; no one can live there" (Leonard, 25).

Robert E. Scholes has written that "every writer's work offers us a different system of notation, which has its focal limits in abstracting from the total system of existence."[4] If, then, each significant writer employs "narrative codes" that illuminate – even elucidate – his or her "version of reality,"[4] then all accomplished representations of such individual world views merit consideration on their own terms. Perhaps the novelist who has made satire her narrative code runs the greatest risk of producing specimens, coolly dissected. Satire, by definition, chronicles folly to the end that institutions may be improved.

Deceit and camouflage are Lurie's enemies, and she attacks their practitioners without remorse. Sometimes, as Joseph Parisi observes, "the very brilliance of her technique becomes cause for dissatisfaction." For all her characters' complexities, he adds, the unmasking process often reduces them to stock figures or Jonsonian humours, cleverly but predictably laid bare for ridicule.[5]

William H. Pritchard, in a brief review of *The War between the Tates*, finds Lurie "so confessedly pulling the strings (now I'm going to have my character do *this*) that it is difficult to look past her manipulative gestures, accomplished as always they are, and believe there's somebody really out there in trouble."[6] Or, as John Leonard puts it, *The War between the Tates* is inhabited by characters who are denied possibility. "Alison Lurie's clamp is on them. . . . It is not their fault that they are limited; it is hers" (Leonard, 25).

"How Good Is Alison Lurie?"

One of the most severe critiques of Lurie's fiction through *The War between the Tates* is John W. Aldridge's "How Good Is Alison Lurie?" Like many other critics, Aldridge does praise Lurie's style and her powers of observation:

> She writes a prose of great clarity and concision, an expository language that efficiently serves her subject but does not stylize upon it. She has many true things to say about the various modes of self-deception and distraction by which we endure the passage of life *in these peculiarly trivializing times*, and she often says them in a manner she has earned entirely by herself and that represents an authentic fictional voice.[7]

He then joins a more select group of reviewers who, even when citing what they perceive to be the virtues of her work, undercut their praise with criticism:

> There is some firm evidence in the five novels she has so far published that Alison Lurie should be a better novelist than she is. Her reputation up to now does not indicate that she has been widely appreciated for the qualities she does possess, although she has acquired over the years a certain small cult following, and . . . *The War between the Tates* appears to be winning her the kind of popular attention which may prove only that her limitations have at last begun to be recognized as seeming more attractive than her virtues. (Aldridge, 79, emphasis added)

The rest of the essay – about four-fifths of it – seeks to demonstrate that what Lurie has chosen to write about is unworthy of her attention and is rendered even less significant by her treatment. Specifically, Aldridge's criticisms include these: (1) She relies too heavily on sexual intrigue to fuel dramatic possibilities, (2) she works the same infidelity plot from book to book, and (3) her treatment of adultery is suggestive of soap opera – insufficiently revelatory for serious fiction. "Her treatment of adultery suffers, in short, from arbitrariness and inconsequence. The insight it affords us into the natures of the people who commit it is finally reducible to some idea of orgasmic liberation, which is repeatedly seen as in and for itself an apocalyptic experience" (Aldridge, 80).

Katharine Rogers has provided the most penetrating defense so far of Lurie's "adultery plot," claiming that its very repetitiousness "enables her to explore varied aspects of her themes of marital discontent and female consciousness-raising" (Rogers, 118). She explains that while Lurie's unfulfilled wives "are not totally conventional . . . none has seriously questioned the fundamental assumptions with which she has been brought up. Although theoretically they had many choices in life, they have acted as if they had none. Having accepted the feminine mystique of the fifties, they devote themselves wholly to their families and expect marriage and children to provide . . . fulfillment" (Rogers, 117).

Thus, what Aldridge regards as a hackneyed plot in which good sex with someone not one's legal spouse "achieves some temporary sense of rejuvenated identity" is for Rogers a passport out of a false sense of self-assurance to a new potential for growth, whose immediate form may be passion, even ecstasy, but whose long-term achievement is self-knowledge. Rogers, a feminist scholar, concludes with the following observations:

> This concern with awakening her heroines to look critically at their lives is what makes Lurie a feminist author. . . . her encouragement of radical questioning, symbolized by the respectable wife's trying out of adultery, is liberating. So, in a lighter way, is her deadly accurate rendition of the irritations and frustrations usual in marriage – obtusely self-centered husbands, ungrateful children for whose deficiencies their mother is made to feel responsible, an endless round of routine tasks, none of which are appreciated. . . . Lurie's adultery plot not only punishes these husbands as they deserve but highlights the husband's obliviousness to his wife's feelings and needs by contrasting it with the lover's attentiveness. The contrast is even sharper in the cases where the husband feels he is entitled to an extramarital affair because his wife is no longer giving him the devotion or excitement he considers his due. (Rogers, 126)

Aldridge also takes exception to the value of the academic scene during the latter half of the century as a vehicle for satire. "Nothing is more obvious to anyone familiar with the university scene of the last twenty years than that the dramatic possibilities for a fiction dealing with academic life are not what they once were" (Aldridge, 81). He goes on to list Mary McCarthy (whom he once savaged in his essay "Mary McCarthy and the Trolls"), Helen Howe, Randall Jarrell, Robie Macauley, and Bernard Malamud as the "classic practitioners" of the novel of academe, saying that Lurie, in comparison, lacks "advantages," none of which he identifies. Nothing is at stake in *The War between the Tates*, he writes – no risk, no threat, no anguish. "The society in which . . . [the Tates] exist is much too limited, drab, and morally diffuse to give them consequence. . . . It is a society made for and by the burgeoning new population of academic Babbitts, and it is the ideal medium for their relentlessly bourgeois pursuit" (Aldridge, 81).

Since the publication of his influential *After the Lost Generation* in 1951, Aldridge has continually denounced American novelists. He is a critic of the postwar scene whose constant refrain is that triviality in society begets triviality in its commentators. Ironically, Lurie shares Aldridge's view of society. His criticism of an ally raises the question of whether a satirical novelist can be faulted because her choice of evidence does not coincide with his.

Late Dividends

The War between the Tates, which rose to the top of the *New York Times* fiction list in the late summer of 1974 and remained there throughout the fall and early winter, was followed by two books quite different in content and theme from her previous efforts. *Only Children* and *Foreign Affairs* are, in craft and language, her best novels to date. On this the major reviews are in agreement. With *Only Children*, it was for the first time her peers among female writers, such as Joyce Carol Oates, Mary Gordon, and Victoria Glendinning, who paid her tribute.

Only Children (1979) embraced an idea Lurie had been nursing for years. She would blend, Proust-like, recovered memories of childhood and her understanding of the workings of children's imaginations with her scholar's knowledge of folklore and children's literature. She was coeditor, with Justin G. Schiller, of the 73-volume *Classics of Children's Literature* (1974-75). After the publication of *Only Children* she compiled three collections of retold stories for children: *The Heavenly Zoo* (1980); *Legends and Tales of the Stars* (1980); and *Fabulous Beasts* (1981).

Neither the Oates nor the Gordon review is a "puff"; each expresses a reservation – Oates on the book's lack of "amusing peripheral characters" evident in earlier works[8] and Gordon on perceived lapses in conveying the tone of childhood (Gordon, 27). Gordon, however, is especially generous to Lurie for her rescue of objects from an all-but-lost past that we still crave and for her sure feel for the often unwitting cruelty adults inflict on their children. Oates also praises *Only Children*'s briskness and verve, a triumph in the comic mode by one "who knows its contours and idiosyncrasies and its meticulous pacing exceptionally well" (Oates, 27).

Glendinning called *Only Children* "a powerful novel. Imaginary friends or real people, her characters live on in the mind. And the clear intellectual framework is effectively embedded in a totally real-ized world of food and clothes and furniture and weather. . . . The indecency of love – which is a classical concept, as this is a classical novel – is most people's lot."[9]

Foreign Affairs, though it did not enjoy the commercial success of *The War between the Tates*, is Lurie's most critically acclaimed novel, both here and abroad. In England, Lorna Sage describes the

novel as "the kind . . . that elicits a conspiratorial glow . . . because it
flatters readers unmercifully" by leaving them "well-buttered with
irony" (Sage, 109). American though she is, Lurie's writing resonates
with the English literary past. Marilyn Butler, writing in the *London
Review of Books*, finds the novel a major advance from the
"programmatic naturalism" of previous books. "The nuanced and
naturalistically-observed middle-aged love-affair between Vinnie and
Chuck shows the kind of writing Lurie still perhaps does best, but
her bold and freely-handled alternative plot enormously widens its
range of suggestion."[10] It is difficult to conceive of an American
novelist writing about London who is not faulted on details by
English critics. Henry James did not escape, and neither does Lurie.
Richard Boston and James Lasdun enumerate a number of gaffes,
none of them substantive.[11]

Among American reviewers, Dorothy Wickenden notes that
Lurie, like most comic writers, relies on startling juxtapositions to
illumine the individual's accommodations to the demands of society.
She judges Lurie "as deft as ever when she turns to the mortifica-
tions of romance. She is an uncannily accurate observer of the
ambivalent emotions that enter into unconventional sexual
alliances. . . . "[12]

The most glowing assessment is Carol Simpson Stern's. She hails
Foreign Affairs as "the best of her novels to date [because of] the
daring way in which it treats (approvingly) Vinnie's affair with a
Western bumpkin from Tulsa, Oklahoma. . . . hardly a suitable candidate for Vinnie's affections."[13] After faulting her previous novels for
being sometimes unconvincing about sexual affairs between different
types of people and lacking John Updike's "genius for sexually
explicit scenes," Stern comes down resoundingly in favor of this
book. Lurie has found "the right ingredients. Not only do we believe
in the sexuality of both characters, but we grow to care very much
for Chuck and Vinnie. This facet . . . is surprising. Lurie's writing is
always witty and tightly controlled, but she is usually best at making
us laugh at, not with, her characters; in this book, we laugh, and
finally cry, with the characters, not at their expense" (Stern, 548).

In *Foreign Affairs*, the reader is invited to glimpse the truth of
Luis de Leon's maxim about the necessity of each person to act in
conformity with nature and business.[14] Vinnie Miner's sense of
herself, fortresslike at the outset of the novel, resists siege and

remains essentially intact. Fred Turner comes to recognize that his nature is to seek reconciliation on the homefront rather than find more enrichment abroad. At the same time, writes Margaret Ezell, *Foreign Affairs* wittily dissects "why we rarely get what we think we see in other people. Lurie takes both our expectations and disappointments and . . . wryly explores disillusionment [and] unexpected pleasures."[15]

Feminist Response to Lurie's Work

Shortly after receiving the Pulitzer Prize for *Foreign Affairs* in 1985, Alison Lurie told a Dallas interviewer, "Someone who reads reviews will get to know what reviewers to trust. They'll know that if their reviewer likes something they'll probably like it too." Of their value to writers, she was more problematical: "A critic who likes your work is on your wavelength and one who doesn't is not. You can't possibly please everyone. And some people you're going to annoy very much" (Satz, 196).

It has been Alison Lurie's fate to have annoyed a few critics and reviewers very much while pleasing the vast majority. Katharine Rogers notwithstanding, feminist critics are among those she has annoyed. Several see her heroines as taking bold steps against oppressive marriages only to retreat in the end. Lurie never permits peremptory action against the husbands; the issues between husband and wife are resolved by a reconciliation (*The War between the Tates*) or by an ambiguous separation (*The Nowhere City*).

Writing in *Ms.*, Rachel B. Cowen finds that Erica Tate's war, while waged against the backdrop of the women's liberation movement, ends in misdirecting its lessons. Erica deploys the weapons and tactics of the movement against Brian while ultimately failing to use them as "tools for developing her own self-awareness."[16] As mentioned earlier, Rogers believes, to the contrary, that it is in the exploration of the development of self-awareness that Lurie excels (Rogers, 12).

Not all of Cowen's charges in "The Bore between the Tates" are based in feminist theory. She objects to Lurie's "caricatures" of the Tates and, even more, to those of their lovers. No single character of Lurie's has evoked more controversy than that of Wendy Gahaghan, the counterculture innocent who, in company with a kindred spirit, heads for Haight-Ashbury carrying her Indian apparel and Brian's child. Cowen protests: "If this were a popular novel written by a man, many feminists would feel justifiable rage at the scornful, stereotypical way her character is portrayed" (Cowen, 42). By dispatching Wendy, Cowen declares, Lurie has taken the easy way out.

Chapter Ten

"The Whole Confusing Contradictory Truth"

"Feminist, but Not Separatist":
The Truth about Lorin Jones

The Truth about Lorin Jones (1988) may never be as important to cultural history as *The War between the Tates*. It is not as consummately crafted as *Foreign Affairs* or *Only Children*. Yet its significance in Alison Lurie's growth as a novelist cannot be overestimated. It may well be a *prolegomenon* – an announcement – of the kind that every novelist of substance delivers from time to time. To say that *The Truth about Lorin Jones* may portend a shift to higher ground is not to diminish Lurie's past achievements, which are considerable, but to credit her with the expectation that her major statements lie ahead; that, as she puts it, "you simply cannot grow by doing the same things, however expert doing them makes you" (Conversation).

The novel chronicles the search by a failed painter named Polly Alter for the truth about the life and death of Lorin Jones (1926-69), a doomed artist. In his review of the novel, Edmund White equated Jones's life with that of the late Diane Arbus,[1] but Lurie states the character is "internally" built on a girl the author knew at Radcliffe who was stricken with schizophrenia at 19 and never recovered.[2]

Polly Alter is well named. Her inquiry into Jones's story will not only alter her perceptions about Lorin Jones but will also alter – in fact, salvage – her own life. Other Lurie heroines have been transformed; but Polly's path toward self-recognition proves to be an altogether more absorbing process.

Lurie has declared herself a feminist, but not a separatist.[3] The distinction between the two adds dramatic conflict to her eighth novel. White goes so far as to declare that on an "intimate level" the hovering tension of the book is whether Polly will "end up a lesbian feminist separatist or remain unregenerate and heterosexual" (White, 3). Lurie's undisguised attack on lesbian feminism looms large in the novel.

At first, in her determination to keep all the cards stacked against the males in her subject's seemingly martyred life, Polly appears to have decided on lesbianism to affirm the courage of her convictions. She enters into a brief and unsatisfactory affair with a separatist friend, Jeanne, who insinuates both herself and, when Polly fails as partner, her lesbian lover into Polly's apartment.

Jeanne's behavior has an effect on Polly opposite to that which Jeanne intends. Her actions and words both speak loudly to end Polly's sexual ambivalence. White writes:

> When Jeanne says that Polly's 14-year-old son is turning into a 'man,' she stresses the word with distaste, as though she were saying "monkey." Jeanne makes suppers of tabbouleh [sic] and cucumber in yogurt, spells out words like c-r-a-p as though a susceptible child were always listening, and turns every space she inhabits into a nest of glossy magazines, ruffled calico aprons, pink cable-knit sweaters, painted teapots and an ashtray in the form of a heart. Jeanne may be a doctrinaire man-hater, but she's in no way opposed to impersonating the old-fashioned, sweet-smelling, suffocating mother. . . . Her rhetoric conceals a scheming, aggressive personality. (White, 3)

Although Polly cannot honestly embrace lesbianism for herself, she is willing to exploit her flirtation with it. "I'm a lesbian,"[4] she declares for the first time in her life, as she jockeys for position at the estate of Garrett Jones, an eminent art critic and patron as well as Lorin's first husband. She repeats the assertion during a promising encounter in Key West with a stranger who will turn out to have been, in an earlier incarnation, a hippie poet and Lorin's last husband (*Lorin Jones*, 248). With both men, Polly's bogus confession of lesbianism is strategic. She uses it as both a sexual put-off and a political turn-on with the two men who can help her most with the biography she is writing.

For two-thirds of the book, Polly reads male stereotyping and the double standard in nearly everything, especially in the world of art, where she failed early as a painter and now must maneuver as a researcher. Lurie knows the art world, particularly its patronage system. If Polly accedes to his sexual advances, Garrett Jones can ease her way. Her employers at the museum will promote her, and the dealer who shows Lorin's work will oversee the favorable reviewing of Polly's book.

Ultimately, however, Polly cannot deceive herself. For a time she is no less prone to self-deception and self-justification than such late-comers to self-discovery as Erica Tate and Vinnie Miner. Although embittered by losses, actual and threatened (her son Steve may decide to stay in Denver, where his father had elected to take a scientific research position at the expense of his marriage to Polly), she cannot in the end deny her own feelings. They express themselves as conflicting voices in her head – Socratic dialogues between herself and Lorin Jones. It is Polly's nature to be fair-minded; she realizes she can neither write nor live by a predetermined agenda that skirts the truth.

Polly is vexed by heterosexual fantasies. "It was an addiction, really," she reflects, when attracted to a man she has met, "like Jeanne's addiction to cigarettes. There ought to be an organization for it, Heterosexuals Anonymous . . . and when the uncontrollable urge came over you, you'd telephone their hotline and some nice woman would talk to you till you felt better" (*Lorin Jones*, 250). Yet what helps bring Polly to the truth about herself is her affair with Hugh Cameron, the one-time hippie poet, now middle-aged, who had been Lorin Jones's husband at the time of her death. Polly's relationship with Cameron, whom she knows at first only as "Mac," proprietor of a business significantly called "Revivals Construction," occupies most of the final third of the novel. It takes place, perhaps also appropriately, in Key West, where Hugh will provide the keys to Lorin's mystery, to Polly's reconstruction and revival, and to the larger theme of the book.

Alison Lurie and the Biographical Fallacy

Externally, the major plot of *The Truth about Lorin Jones* is devoted to the caprices of seeking – and failing to find – substantiating evidence for a psychobiography that is in accord with the biographer's bias. Polly Alter's original agenda is to demonstrate how Lorin Jones was an underrated genius exploited and driven into an early

death by her unsatisfying career and the men in her life. These
include her dealer; her half-brother, the ubiquitous L. D. Zimmern,
noted only twice in this book as the legal owner of Lorin's unsold
paintings; her first husband, art critic and historian Garrett Jones,
inveterate womanizer; and, finally, Hugh Cameron, who spirited
Lorin away to Key West only to abandon her – apparently – when she
was ill and dying.

The novel alternates long chapters – how Polly sees aspects of
what she infers as Lorin's angst as intersecting her own – with short
chapters in the words of the surviving intimates and associates of the
artist. Reading the novel becomes an exercise in ferreting out unreliable narrators until one learns the lesson every serious biographer
comes to know. There is no "truth" about persons like Lorin Jones,
only impressions of truth:

> None of the people Polly had interviewed were lying, not wholly anyhow:
> Everyone had told her the truth as he or she knew or imagined it. All they
> agreed on was that Lorin was beautiful and gifted. . . . Otherwise, everyone
> seemed to have known a different Lorin Jones; and most of them had different
> versions of other people in Lorin's life. . . . She had found out too much.
> How . . . to make sense of it all? (*Lorin Jones*, 320)

Although the influence of Henry James may be at work in *The
Truth about Lorin Jones* (White finds a precedent in *The Bostonians*,
James's attack on feminism, in which Olive Chancellor and Basil
Ransom struggle for the soul of Verena Tarrant [White, 37]), James
may not provide the truest paradigm here. Thematically, *The Truth
about Lorin Jones* is closer to Somerset Maugham's ironic comedy,
Cakes and Ale. The two books are alike in their exposure of the folly
of appearances. Maugham's Willie Ashenden, like Polly Alter, rebels
against the opportunism of taking a one-dimensional view of genius.
The lives of Maugham's Edward Driffield and Lurie's Lorin Jones are
equally resistant to easy answers to troubling questions. Although
many are called to testify, it is the characters rated lowest by the
would-be biographers – namely, Driffield's first wife, the barmaid
Rosie Gann, and Lorin Jones's second husband, Hugh Cameron – who have touched the subjects' lives most truly. They made it
possible for the stifled creative geniuses of novelist and painter,
respectively, to flower after earlier adversity.

In Lurie's fictional world, wisdom is earned only after persistent difficulties. Polly's morality tale blurs with each successive play of her tape recorder. Lorin's "faults and merits vary according to the observer [and] we also see how the witnesses all have a vested interest in how the story will be told. . . . [while] all variously praise and malign one another" (White, 3).

One of the strengths of the novel is how clearly Lorin comes across, even though we never hear her voice directly. For Lurie fans, the poignancy of Lorin's story and her death at 43 is intensified by the memory of her as eight-year-old Lolly Zimmern in *Only Children*. The shadows cast over the vampire-fearing little girl lengthened as she grew up, as *The Truth about Lorin Jones* reveals. The spirits that haunted Lolly stayed with her until her death more than three decades later.

Nor should readers be surprised that Dan Zimmern, the Madison Avenue wheeler-dealer of *Only Children*, treated his daughter dotingly and indulgently, or that Danielle Zimmern, divorced wife of L. D. Zimmern and best friend of Erica in *The War between the Tates*, makes a return appearance as Lorin's sister-in-law. She faults Lorin for never learning to stand on her own feet or consulting a psychiatrist. We learn that Lorin married an adoring critic because she knew he could advance her career. When his advice about her work became threatening, she discarded him for Hugh Cameron.

Near the end of the novel, Polly collates the unruly pages of her subject's life, but the collation only increases her perplexity. "There was the shy little girl Lolly Zimmern; the flaky college freshman Laurie; the bohemian art student . . . the neurotic, unworldly artist. There was the poetic lost child Laura whom Garrett Jones had married, and the obsessed genius who had died at Key West. According to her niece, Lorin was generous and sensitive; her stepmother remembered her as selfish and spiteful" (*Lorin Jones*, 320).

Alison Lurie: An Afterword

Polly Alter faces the quandary of every biographer. Now that she has thoroughly "researched" the life of Lorin Jones, what sort of account should she – dare she – write? What kind of genius should her book portray: an innocent victim or a narcissistic ingrate? Either way, given all she has learned, Polly knows that partial truths end up being collective lies. "What she'd really like to do . . . was to write a book that would tell the whole confusing contradictory truth. She'd like to put in all the different stories she'd collected, and – as her father used to say – let the devil take the hindmost" (*Lorin Jones*, 324). The whole confusing contradictory truth: not a bad description for the world Alison Lurie faces as a novelist in the 1990s. What sort of novel should she – dare she – write?

To date Lurie has been productive, publishing a novel every three to five years for the past 30 years. And what she has produced has been finely crafted. Even a critic such as John Aldridge, who gives the impression of having read everything in American literature since World War II and liked almost none of it, acknowledges that Lurie writes both beautifully and brilliantly. She writes with lucidity and economy; her tone is appropriate to her material, rarely false.

Lurie is a probing satirist who sees self-deception as the handiwork of a culture facing bankruptcy, and nowhere more so than in the domestic realm. No American writer has more searchingly unveiled the agonies of women trapped in patriarchy. No one reading the opening chapters of *The War between the Tates* and its spiritual forebear, *Love and Friendship*, can doubt that for Lurie's generation of college-reared women it was not only men who lived lives of quiet desperation.

Although 35 years old when her first novel was published, Lurie must be seen as a novelist in progress. It is to her credit that the three books since *The War between the Tates* have been much less like this central work than three of the four preceding it. This pattern of innovation can be seen best in terms of technique. *Only Children* requires interplay between innocence and experience. *Foreign Affairs* mounts a double plot that looks ahead to the sophisticated multiple perspectives of *The Truth about Lorin Jones*. *The War between the Tates* requires an immediacy of narrative delivery almost equivalent to communiqués from a war zone. *Only Children* and *Foreign Affairs* render Jamesian strategies of viewpoint more amenable to comedy. The former plays the timeless world of children against the more problematic anxieties of time-bound grown-ups. The latter installs for the first time in a Lurie novel a zoom-lens consciousness that does much of the reader's thinking. Lurie has crossed George Eliot's supplemental authorial voice with late-Henry James central intelligence.

In the thirteenth chapter of *The French Lieutenant's Woman*, John Fowles parodies both traditional and postmodernist fiction by stopping the action and setting his characters free of their creator's intentions. Ironically, Fowles becomes even more manipulative from that point, but he seems to have been serious when he wrote that "it is only when our characters and events begin to disobey us that they begin to live."[5] *The Truth about Lorin Jones* is the least programmatic of Lurie's eight novels. The ending is the most open ended. On the last page of the novel Polly indicates she feels like someone who has just come up from underwater. It is apparent that her creator is no more certain about her fate than Polly is.

One might wish for more uncharted fates in the novels that follow *The Truth about Lorin Jones*. To Alison Lurie's gifts of intelligence, sharp observant comedy, and wry puncturing of pretense there could then be added the ability to convey inconsistency and unpredictability, ingredients so characteristic of contemporary life.

Appendix

The Recurrence of L. D. Zimmern in Lurie's Novels

Alison Lurie cites English novelist Anthony Powell as a "major influence because of all those recurring characters in his *Music of Time* novels" (Conversation). While Powell's elaborate weaving in and out of characters from book to book is not typical of Lurie, it is noteworthy that one character, known as Lennie, Leonard, or L. D. Zimmern, appears in Lurie's last five novels.

"That's a private joke," Lurie notes. "Zimmern is the protagonist of the first novel I ever wrote – one of the two I couldn't get published. Now I keep bringing him in as a sort of reminder that he was vital to my first efforts at fiction" (Conversation).

Except for *The Truth about Lorin Jones*, in which we learn that the child we knew as Lolly Zimmern in *Only Children* grew up to be catastrophe-prone painter Lorin Jones, there is no other instance of Lurie's fictionally tracing a character from one novel to another as he or she ages. What follows is a review of Zimmern's appearances in Lurie's work.

Lennie Zimmern in *Only Children* is something of a fifth wheel. The child of Dan Zimmern's first marriage, Lennie is uncomfortable with his father, whom he hates, and out of sync with him and his second wife throughout the long Independence Day weekend. "Fourteen years old and a real meanie" – eight-year-old Mary Ann Hubbard's description – Lennie is untrustworthy with firecrackers and given to scaring his half-sister Lolly with Dracula stories. His precocity cannot be doubted, but it serves his darker side.

Nearly three decades later, in the mid-1960s, Leonard Zimmern figures in *Real People* as an interloper among the creative writers, artists, and composers who attend the Yaddo-like colony at Illyria. Characterized by protagonist Janet Belle Smith as "the intellectual looking man with the horn-rimmed glasses," Zimmern is supposedly finishing a book on the self in contemporary American literature. He is unpopular among the fiction writers because of his reputation as a literary executioner. "Having him at Illyria is like letting a hunter into a wildlife sanctuary," complains a burned-out novelist named Charlie Baxter. Zimmern and the sculptor Nick Donato jointly speculate on which of the women at the colony they can seduce. Leonard thus becomes privy to Janet's affair with Nick.

L. D. Zimmern is the divorced husband of Erica's best friend, Danielle, in *The War between the Tates*. We learn that he joined the English faculty of Corinth University in 1964, at 43. When Brian Tate has his affair and he and his wife, Erica, temporarily separate, Zimmern frequently offers Brian advice on the politics of divorce. In 1969 Zimmern's reputation as a scholar is approaching its zenith, and he gets a chair at Columbia University.

By the early 1980s, the time frame of *Foreign Affairs*, L. D. Zimmern is a regular contributor to magazines such as the *Atlantic*, in whose pages he savages Vinnie Miner's research on children's playground songs. Zimmern is now in his early sixties. His daughter Ruth (Roo) Zimmern Turner is the young wife of Fred Turner, the other protagonist, who is also in London on a grant.

Finally, Leonard Zimmern makes two brief appearances in *The Truth about Lorin Jones* as the owner of his late half-sister's embattled paintings. Lurie's private joke notwithstanding, Zimmern can claim little else from readers but a certain cold intellectual respect.

Notes and References

Chapter One

1. "No One Asked Me to Write a Novel," *New York Times Book Review*, 6 June 1982, 13; hereafter cited in text as "No One Asked."

2. Bradley Phillips, Introduction to *V. R. Lang: Poems & Plays* (New York: Random House, 1975), unpaginated; hereafter cited in text as *Lang*.

3. Unpublished conversation with author, 21 September 1989, at Ithaca, New York; hereafter cited in text as Conversation.

4. Jay Parini, "The Novelist at Sixty," *Horizon* 29 (March 1986): 22.

5. Sara Sanborn, review of *The War between the Tates*, *New York Times Book Review*, 28 July 1974, 1; hereafter cited in text.

Chapter Two

1. *The War between the Tates* (New York: Random House, 1974), 237; hereafter cited in text as *The Tates*.

2. Tony Tanner, *Adultery in the Novel: Contract and Transgression* (Baltimore and London: Johns Hopkins University Press, 1979), 16; hereafter cited in text.

3. Jane Miller, *Women Writing about Men* (New York: Pantheon, 1986), 2-3.

4. Robert A. Donovan, *The Shaping Vision: Imagination in the English Novel from Defoe to Dickens* (Ithaca: Cornell University Press, 1966), 56.

5. Quoted in Katharine M. Rogers, "Alison Lurie: The Uses of Adultery," in *American Women Writing Fiction: Memory, Identity, Family, Space*, ed. Mickey Pearlman (Lexington: University of Kentucky Press, 1989), 115; hereafter cited in text.

6. George Eliot, *Middlemarch* (Boston: Houghton Mifflin/Riverside Editions, ed. and intr. Gordon S. Haight, 1956), 144.

7. Henry James, *The Portrait of a Lady* (Boston: Houghton Mifflin/Riverside Editions, ed. Leon Edel, 1963), 482.

8. A. O. J. Cockshut, *Man and Woman: A Study of Love and the Novel, 1740-1940* (New York: Oxford University Press, 1978), 125; hereafter cited in text.

9. H. G. Wells, *Tono-Bungay* (Boston: Houghton Mifflin/Riverside Editions, ed. Bernard Bergonzi, 1966), 150.

Chapter Three

1. *Love and Friendship* (New York: Macmillan, 1962), 313; hereafter cited in text as *L&F*.

2. William Dean Howells, *The Rise of Silas Lapham* (New York: Holt, Rinehart & Winston, 1966), 257; hereafter cited in text.

3. Gertrude Stein, *Everybody's Autobiography* (New York: Cooper Square, 1971), 289.

4. *The Nowhere City* (New York: Avon, 1965), 118; hereafter cited in text.

5. *London Times Literary Supplement,* 4 February 1965, 81.

6. Lester Goldberg (author of *In Siberia It Is Very Cold,* [New York: Dembner Books, 1987]), in letter to author, 30 November 1989.

7. Lurie refers to *The Good Soldier* as a "masterpiece." (See her essay on Ford Madox Ford in *Don't Tell the Grown-ups: Subversive Children's Literature* [Boston: Little, Brown & Co., 1990], 75). Dowell, the narrator, shares with Mary Belle Smith the limitations of first-person viewpoint. Dowell's impairments as narrator install the overriding question, "How can we know what is itself true?" as what *The Good Soldier* is about.

8. *Real People* (New York: Avon, 1969), 14; hereafter cited in text.

9. H. Porter Abbott, *Diary Fiction: Writing as Action* (Ithaca: Cornell University Press, 1984), 41.

10. George Orwell, "Writers and Leviathan," in *Orwell's 'Nineteen Eighty-Four': Text, Sources, Criticism*, ed. Irving Howe (San Diego: Harcourt Brace Jovanovich, 1982), 414.

Chapter Four

1. I am indebted to Julian Jebb for this extended analogy. See note 5 for full citation and direct quotes.

2. William Shakespeare, *King Henry IV* (Part 1), act 5, scene 1.

3. For an explication of how profoundly Lurie has made a subtext of George Kennan's writings, see Judie Newman, "Sexual and Civil Conflicts: George F. Kennan and *The War between the Tates,*" chap. 5 in *University Fiction*, 103-22, ed. David Bevan (London: Rodopi Perspectives on Modern Literature, 1990); hereafter cited in text.

4. Phoebe Adams, review of *The War between the Tates, Atlantic,* September 1974, 103.

5. Julian Jebb, review of *The War between the Tates, London Magazine,* December 1974/January 1975, 127; hereafter cited in text.

6. Martha Satz, "A Kind of Detachment: An Interview with Alison Lurie," *Southwest Review* 71 (Spring 1986): 196; hereafter cited in text.

7. Michael S. Helfand, "The Dialectic of Self and Community in Alison Lurie's *The War between the Tates*," *Perspectives on Contemporary Literature* 3 (1977): 69.

8. Amanda Smith, "David Lodge," *Publishers Weekly*, 18 August 1989, 41.

9. Roger Sale, "The Way We Live Now," review of *The War between the Tates, New York Review of Books*, 8 August 1974, 34.

Chapter Five

1. David Lehman, "A Kind of Witchery," *Newsweek*, 24 September 1984, 80; hereafter cited in text.

2. Richard Ellmann, *James Joyce* (New York: Oxford University Press, 1982), 149.

3. Mary Gordon, review of *Only Children, New York Review of Books*, 14 June 1979, 32; hereafter cited in text.

4. *Only Children* (New York: Random House, 1979), 240; hereafter cited in text.

5. *Don't Tell the Grown-ups: Subversive Children's Literature* (Boston: Little, Brown & Co., 1990), 9; hereafter cited in text as *Grown-ups*.

6. Henry James, preface to *What Maisie Knew*, in *The Art of the Novel: Critical Prefaces*, ed. R. P. Blackmur (New York: Scribners, 1962), 146.

7. *Foreign Affairs* (New York: Random House, 1984), 115; hereafter cited in text.

8. Dale Edmonds, "The World Seemed So Empty to Me If I Wasn't Writing," interview with Alison Lurie, *Negative Capability* 6, no. 4 (Fall 1986): 160.

9. Michiko Kakutani, "The Rebellious Heroes of Children's Classics," *New York Times*, 27 February 1990, B2.

10. Rosellen Brown, "Once Upon a Time: The Real Story," *New York Times Book Review*, 11 March 1990, 13.

11. Jack K. Campbell, paper presented at the International Society for Educational Biography, Toronto, Canada, May 1989.

12. Quoted in Jack K. Campbell, "The Quest of the Historical Child," *Review Journal of Philosophy & Social Science* (Meerut, India: ANU Books 9, no. 1 [1984]): 13.

Chapter Six

1. Leon Edel, *Henry James: A Life* (New York: Harper & Row, 1985), 534.

2. Henry James, *The Ambassadors,* with introductions by Martin W. Sampson and John C. Gerber (New York: Harper & Row, 1930), 149.

3. Lorna Sage, "Adventures in the Old World," *London Times Literary Supplement,* 1 February 1985, 109; hereafter cited in text.

4. Rebecca West, *There Is No Conversation,* in her *The Harsh Voice: Four Short Novels* (Garden City, N.J.: Doubleday, Doran, 1935), 67.

5. Henry James, preface to *The Ambassadors,* in *The Art of the Novel: Critical Prefaces,* ed. R. P. Blackmur (New York: Scribners, 1962), 321.

Chapter Seven

1. David Jackson, "An Interview with Alison Lurie," *Shenandoah* 31, 4 (1980): 17; hereafter cited in text.

2. *The Language of Clothes* (New York: Random House, 1981), 261; hereafter cited in text as *Clothes.*

3. H. G. Wells and Lurie, nonspecialists, respectively, in world history and clothing, were praised for their comprehensive studies by intelligent generalists, who appreciated their readability, but discounted by specialists.

4. J. D. Reed, review of *The Language of Clothes, Time,* 30 November 1981, 96; hereafter cited in text.

5. Walter Goodman, review of *The Language of Clothes, New York Times,* 17 January 1982, 16.

6. Anne Hollander, "Rags," review of *The Language of Clothes, New York Review of Books,* 15 April 1982, 38; hereafter cited in text as Hollander.

7. Reeves, a promising romantic actor in films before World War II, put on much weight in the service and never again achieved the roles he wanted. As television's first Superman, he became typecast, and by the time of his suicide in June 1959 he was reduced to seeking carnival billing as a wrestler.

Chapter Eight

1. "The Woman Who Rode Away," review of John Updike's *Trust Me: Short Stories* and *S., New York Review of Books,* 12 May 1988, 3.

2. Roger Zimmern bears only a distant relationship to L. D. Zimmern – "perhaps a remote cousin," according to Lurie (Conversation).

3. Judie Newman, "Alison Lurie," *Post-war Literatures in English* (December 1990): 6; hereafter cited in text.

4. *Imaginary Friends* (New York: Avon, 1968), 77; hereafter cited in text.

5. Irving Malin, review of *Imaginary Friends, Commonweal* 87 (12 January 1968): 454.

Chapter Nine

1. John Skow, review of *The War between the Tates, Time*, 29 July 1974, 64.

2. David Lehman, "A Kind of Witchery," *Newsweek*, 24 September 1984, 80.

3. John Leonard, review of *The War between the Tates, New Republic*, 10 August 1974, 25; hereafter cited in the text.

4. Robert E. Scholes, coauthor with Eric S. Rabkin, *Science Fiction: History, Science, Vision* (New York: Oxford University Press, 1977), 23.

5. Joseph Parisi, untitled entry, *Contemporary Novelists* (New York: St. Martin's Press, 1982), unpaginated.

6. William H. Pritchard, review of *The War between the Tates, Hudson Review* 28 (Spring 1975): 152.

7. John W. Aldridge, review of *The War between the Tates, Commentary* 59 (January 1975): 79; hereafter cited in text.

8. Joyce Carol Oates, review of *Only Children, New York Times Book Review*, 22 April 1979, 27; hereafter cited in text.

9. Victoria Glendinning, "Putting Away Childish Things," review of *Only Children, Book World, Washington Post*, 29 April 1979, M5.

10. Marilyn Butler, "Amor Vincit Vinnie," *London Review of Books*, 21 February 1985, 5-6.

11. Richard Boston, review of *Foreign Affairs, Punch* 288, no. 7520 (23 January 1985): 52; James Lasdun, review of *Foreign Affairs, Encounter* 65, no. 2 (July-August 1985): 47-51.

12. Dorothy Wickenden, review of *Foreign Affairs, New Republic*, 8 October 1984, 34-36.

13. Carol Simpson Stern, untitled entry, *Contemporary Novelists*, 4th ed. (New York: St. Martin's Press, 1986), 548; hereafter cited in text.

14. Quoted in W. Somerset Maugham, *The Summing Up*, in *The Maugham Reader* (Garden City, N.Y.: Doubleday & Co., 1950), 682.

15. Margaret Ezell, review of *Foreign Affairs*, in "Zest," *Houston Chronicle*, 25 November 1985, 40.

16. Rachel B. Cowen, "The Bore between the Tates," *Ms.*, January 1975, 41; hereafter cited in text.

Chapter Ten

1. Edmund White, "A Victim of the Male Establishment," review of *The Truth about Lorin Jones, New York Times Book Review*, 4 September 1988, 3; hereafter cited in text.

2. Alison Lurie told me in conversation that her classmate would probably have become famous in the same way as the fictional Lorin Jones had she not become ill. Externally, she added, Lorin is a composite of

Helen Frankenthaler, Jane Freilither, and Lee Krasner, who was the wife of Jackson Pollock.

3. See "Research for a Love Affair," a brief sidebar to Edmund White's *NYTBR* review (see note 1). Sarah Ferrell quotes Lurie as believing "that the impulse toward creating a separate world for women, although understandable, is dangerous because of the risk that it will become a second-class world." More recently she elaborated to interviewer Abby Ellis ("Making Her Mark: An Interview with Alison Lurie," *Bloomsbury Review,* March/April 1990, 11): "My thinking has always been that women and men must always keep in contact. I've known women who have really ruled men out of their lives completely. I understand that this can happen, but I think it is something that most of us should question. In the first place, if we turn ourselves off from men, how are we ever going to let them argue or discuss things with us? Or let them know how we're feeling? It deprives both sexes of the chance to communicate."

4. *The Truth about Lorin Jones* (Boston: Little, Brown & Co., 1988), 129; hereafter cited in text as *Lorin Jones.*

5. John Fowles, *The French Lieutenant's Woman* (New York: Signet/New American Library, 1969), 81.

Selected Bibliography

PRIMARY SOURCES

In 1969 Alison Lurie presented drafts and working notes of her books to the Schlesinger Library, Radcliffe College, Cambridge, Massachusetts – her alma mater. This collection – the Alison Lurie Papers – had not been processed at the time this book was completed. The holdings may be viewed upon request.

Fiction

Love and Friendship. New York: Macmillan, 1962; Avon Books, 1962.

The Nowhere City. New York: Coward, 1965; Avon Books, 1967, 1986.

Imaginary Friends. New York: Coward, 1967; Avon Books, 1968, 1986, 1991.

Real People. New York: Random House, 1969; Avon Books, 1969.

The War between the Tates. New York: Random House, 1974; Avon Books, 1975, 1991.

Only Children. New York: Random House, 1979; Avon Books, 1990.

Clever Gretchen and Other Forgotten Folktales (juvenile). New York: Crowell, 1980.

The Heavenly Zoo (juvenile). New York: Farrar, Straus & Giroux, 1980.

Fabulous Beasts (juvenile). New York: Farrar, Straus & Giroux, 1981.

Foreign Affairs. New York: Random House, 1984; Avon Books, 1985, 1990.

The Truth about Lorin Jones. Boston: Little, Brown & Co., 1988; Avon Books, 1990.

"Fat People," *Vogue,* October 1989, 438-39, 466, 468, 470, 472. (This is the first short story Alison Lurie had published in more than 30 years.)

Nonfiction

V. R. Lang: A Memoir. Privately printed, 1959.

V. R. Lang: A Memoir (published in *V. R. Lang: Poems & Plays*). New York: Random House, 1975.

With Justin G. Schiller. *Classics of Children's Literature, 1631-1932 Series.* New York: Garland Publishing, 1977.

The Language of Clothes. New York: Random House, 1981.

Don't Tell the Grown-ups: Subversive Children's Literature. Boston: Little, Brown & Co., 1990; Avon Books, 1991.

Essays and Articles

"Back to Pooh Corner." In *Children's Literature 2*, edited by Francelia Butler, 11-17 (Journal of the Modern Language Association Seminar on Children's Literature and the Children's Literature Association). Philadelphia: Temple University Press, 1973.

"A Tail of Terror." *New York Review of Books*, 11 December 1975, 26.

"Bunny Lang: Death among Friends" (excerpt from *V. R. Lang: Poems & Plays*, with a memoir by Alison Lurie). *Ms.*, December 1975, 118.

"Fairy Tales for a Liberated Age." *Horizon* 19 (July 1977): 80-85.

"Beatrix Potter: More than Just Peter Rabbit." *Ms.*, September 1977, 42-43.

"Braking for Elves." *New York Review of Books*, 8 March 1979, 16-19.

"Vulgar, Coarse and Grotesque." *Harper's*, December 1979, 66-68.

"Return of the Ship of Fools." *New Republic*, 30 August 1980, 17-18.

"Classics of Children's Literature." In *Children's Literature 10*, edited by A. Moss (Annual of the Modern Language Association Group on Children's Literature and the Children's Literature Association). New Haven: Yale University Press, 1980-1984.

"Ford Madox Ford's Fairy Tales." In *Children's Literature 8*, 7-21 (Annual of the Modern Language Association Group on Children's Literature and the Children's Literature Association). New Haven: Yale University Press, 1980-1984.

"Sex and Fashion" (excerpt from *The Language of Clothes*). *New York Review of Books*, 22 October 1981, 38-46.

"No One Asked Me to Write a Novel: The Making of a Writer." *New York Times Book Review*, 6 June 1982, 13, 46-48.

"The Steamy Side of Paradise." *House and Garden*, June 1983, 30.

"The Benevolent Tower." *House and Garden*, September 1984, 174-75.

"E. Nesbit: Riding the Wave of the Future." *New York Review of Books*, 25 October 1984, 19-22.

"On the Road to Timbuktu: Exploring the Strange and Haunting Landscape of Mali." *House and Garden*, September 1985, 46-50.

"Common Courtesy: In Which Miss Manners Solves the Problem That Baffled Mr. Jefferson." *New York Times Book Review*, 10 November 1985, 13.

"To the Manner Born" (British fashion). *New York Times Magazine*, 24 August 1986, S150.

Introduction to *Peter Pan* by James M. Barrie. New York: Signet Classics, 1987.

"Underground Artist: The Children's Books of William Mayne." *New York Review of Books*, 18 February 1988, 11-13.

"A Moody Retreat under Italy's Alps." *New York Times*, 3 April 1988, XX13.

"The Frog Prince." *New York Review of Books,* 24 November 1988, 33-34.
"E. Nesbit." In *Writers for Children,* edited by Jane M. Bingham, 423-30. New York: Scribners, 1988.
"A Dictionary for Deconstructors." *New York Review of Books,* 23 November 1989, 49-50.

Book Reviews

Shardik by Richard Adams. *New York Review of Books,* 12 June 1975, 34.

On Human Finery by Quentin Bell; *Dress and Society, 1560-1970* by G. Squire; *Hollywood Costume – Glamour! Glitter! Romance!* by D. McConathy. *New York Review of Books,* 25 November 1976, 17.

The Book of Merlyn: The Unpublished Conclusion to "The Once and Future King" by T. H. White. *New York Review of Books,* 24 November 1977, 3.

Animals and Men: Their Relationship as Reflected in Western Art from Prehistory to the Present Day by Kenneth Clark; *Freaks: Myths and Images of the Secret Self* by Leslie Fiedler; and *A Fiedler Reader* by Leslie Fiedler. *New York Review of Books,* 23 March 1978, 22.

The Woman's Dress for Success Book by J. T. Malloy; *Seeing through Clothes* by A. Hollander; *In Fashion: Dress in the Twentieth Century* by P. Glynn; *Mirror, Mirror: A Social History of Fashion* by M. and A. Batterberry; and *Avedon: Photographs, 1947-1977* by R. Avedon with an essay by Harold Brodkey. *New York Review of Books,* 7 December 1978, 25.

The World Guide to Gnomes, Fairies, Elves and Other Little People by T. Keighttley; *A Field Guide to the Little People* by N. Arrowsmith and G. Moore; *Gnomes* by W. Huygen and R. Poortvliet; *Faeries* by B. Froud and A. Lee, edited by D. Larkin; *The Fairies in Tradition and Literature* by K. Briggs; *An Encyclopedia of Fairies: Hobgoblins, Brownies, Bogies and Other Supernatural Creatures* by K. Briggs; and *Fairy Tales and After: From Snow White to E. B. White* by R. Sale. *New York Review of Books,* 8 March 1979, Lurie correction. *New York Review of Books,* 3 May 1979, 46.

Kate Greenaway by R. Engen. *New York Review of Books,* 18 March 1982, 15.

American Beauty by L. W. Banner and *Skin to Skin* by P. Glynn. *New York Review of Books,* 2 June 1983, 20.

Oxford Book of Children's Verse in America. New York Times Book Review, 5 May 1985, 16.

The Singing Game by Iona and Peter Opie. *New York Review of Books,* 24 October 1985, 35.

The Good Terrorist and *The Diaries of Jane Somers: The Diary of a Good Neighbor* and *If the Old Could* by Doris Lessing. *New York Review of Books,* 19 December 1985, 8.

"Petals Personified" (review of *The Court of Flora* by J. J. Grandville). *Art and Antiques,* July 1986.

"Roly-poly Fun and Feasting" (review of *The Random House Book of Mother Goose*). *New York Times Book Review,* 9 November 1986, 37.

"True Confessions" (review of *How I Grew* by Mary McCarthy). *New York Review of Books,* 11 June 1987, 19-21.

"The Woman Who Rode Away" (review of *Trust Me: Short Stories* by John Updike). *New York Review of Books,* 12 May 1988, 3-4.

"The Cabinet of Dr. Seuss" (review essay on the works of Dr. Seuss). *New York Review of Books,* 20 December 1990, 50-52.

SECONDARY SOURCES

Interviews

Bannon, Barbara A. *"PW* Interview: Alison Lurie." *Publishers Weekly,* 19 August 1974, 6.

Edmonds, Dale. "Meet the Author: An Interview with Alison Lurie." *Negative Capability,* Fall 1986, 152-59.

Ellis, Abby. "Making Her Mark: An Interview with Alison Lurie." *Bloomsbury Review,* March/April 1990, 11, 18.

Hite, Molly. "Interview with Alison Lurie." *Belles Lettres* 2 (July/August 1987): 9.

Jackson, David. "An Interview with Alison Lurie." *Shenandoah* 31, no. 4 (1980): 15-27.

Lehman, David. "A Kind of Witchery." *Newsweek,* 24 September 1984, 80.

Morris, James McGrath. "Pulitzer Winner Alison Lurie: Still 'Driven to Writing.' " *Washington Post,* 25 April 1985, B12.

Parini, Jay. "The Novelist at Sixty." *Horizon,* March 1986, 21-22.

Satz, Martha. "A Kind of Detachment: An Interview with Alison Lurie." *Southwest Review,* Spring 1986, 194-202.

Parts of Books, Articles, and Reviews

Abbott, H. Porter. *Diary Fiction: Writing as Action.* Ithaca: Cornell University Press, 1984, 40-53. Author uses *Real People* as his model for diary fiction in which the text, in effect, corrects itself. Janet Belle Smith's diary, in Lurie's hands, becomes a technique for revealing Janet's tendency, in life and art, to falsehood and constriction.

Ackroyd, Peter. "Miss American Pie." *Spectator,* 29 June 1974, 807. Excerpts reprinted in *Contemporary Literary Criticism,* vol. 4, 305. Detroit: Gale

Research, 1975. Sees Lurie's *The War betwen the Tates* as owing more to Thurber than to the Vietnam war and finds it "defines contemporary America with lucidity and with charm."

Aldridge, John W. "How Good Is Alison Lurie?" *Commentary*, January 1975, 79-81. Excerpts reprinted in *Contemporary Literary Criticism*, vol. 4, 260-61. Detroit: Gale Research, 1975. While acknowledging Lurie's stylistic capability, Aldridge finds academic life since World War II banal and insignificant and faults Lurie for an imagination he finds inescapably trapped amid clichés.

Bernays, Anne. "What to Think about Chuck and Vinnie." *New York Times Book Review*, 16 September 1984, 9. Excerpts reprinted in *Contemporary Literary Criticism*, vol. 39, 177-78. Detroit: Gale Research, 1986. Finds *Foreign Affairs*, although an "intelligent" novel, crudely manipulated as if "the author as director was unwilling to leave the stage when the curtain goes up."

Champlin, Charles. Review of *Foreign Affairs, Los Angeles Times Book Review*, 21 October 1984, 1, 12. Excerpts reprinted in *Contemporary Literary Criticism*, vol. 39, 181. Detroit: Gale Research, 1986. Finds Lurie "wonderful, sharp and satiric" about London, but "the whole [of *Foreign Affairs*] lacks the vigor of the parts."

Conarroe, Joel. "Footnotes to Lovenotes." *Book World, Washington Post*, 30 September 1984, 6. Excerpts reprinted in *Contemporary Literary Criticism*, vol. 39, 178-79. Detroit: Gale Research, 1986. Despite "a C-minus for accuracy," *Foreign Affairs* is seen to earn points for literateness, wit, and ironic discourse.

Cowen, Rachel B. "The Bore between the Tates." *Ms.*, January 1975, 41-42. A doctrinaire feminist reading of *The War between the Tates* in which Cowen deplores Erica Tate's use of the gains of the woman's movement to punish her husband rather to foster her own self-development.

Gordon, Mary. "What Mary Ann Knew." *New York Review of Books*, 14 June 1979, 31-32. Gordon finds a Proustian dimension in *Only Children*, a rescue of the feel of childhood, which, in fictional terms, is always problematical. Lauds Lurie on the "generosity" of her comedy about domestic life.

Helfand, Michael S. "The Dialectic of Self and Community in Alison Lurie's *The War between the Tates*." In *Perspectives on Contemporary Literature*, vol. 3 (November 1977): 65-70. An occasionally brilliant analysis of an unorthodox subtext in *The War between the Tates*. Helfand goes beyond the realism of Lurie's depiction of a broken marriage to find a complex explanation of the weakness of modern liberalism. Generally insightful, but truncated at end.

Jebb, Julian. "Ordinary Life." *London Magazine*, December 1974/January 1975, 125-28. Excerpts reprinted in *Contemporary Literary Criticism*, vol. 5, 259-60. Detroit: Gale Research, 1976. This British critic places Lurie and *The War between the Tates* above more inventive novelists such as Roth, Mailer, Updike, and Vonnegut for her "sophisticated directness."

Lehmann-Haupt, Christopher. Review of *Foreign Affairs*. *New York Times*, 13 September 1984, C21. Excerpts reprinted in *Contemporary Literary Criticism*, vol. 39, 177. Detroit: Gale Research, 1986. This demanding reviewer awards *Foreign Affairs* and Lurie a perfect 10 – for treatment of classic themes, "marvelous language," her painterly London, her alchemical transmuting of catastrophe into comedy, and deft treading of the fine line between the pathetic and the ridiculous.

Leonard, John. "Recent Notable Fiction: *The War between the Tates*." *New Republic*, 10/17 August 1974, 24-25. Excerpts reprinted in *Contemporary Literary Criticism*, vol. 4, 306-7. Detroit: Gale Research, 1975. Leonard seems to regret having to write that "this marvelously polished, splendidly crafted novel creates an antiseptic space in the mind; no one can live there."

Newman, Judie. "The Revenge of the Trance Maiden: Intertextuality and Alison Lurie." In *Plotting Change: Contemporary Women's Fiction*, edited by Linda Anderson, 113-27 (London: Edward Arnold, 1990). Newman locates all the elements of the mythic "trance maiden" in Verena Roberts, the spiritualist heroine of *Imaginary Friends*. This is a searching feminist reading of Lurie's third novel.

――――. "Alison Lurie." *Post-war Literatures in English*, vol. 10 (1990): 1-14. Newman's British overview of the Lurie oeuvre provides clues to her extraordinary popularity in England and France. Erica Tate, punningly, becomes for Newman's purposes the *Am-Erican state*, and the title of Lurie's best-known novel, the War between the States. This scholar-critic hints that Lurie's portrayals of campus life hit too close to home for her novels to attract major academic attention in the United States but that her un-hectoring tone, unlike that of a Bellow or Mailer, attracts the sort of literate reader who looks for moral seriousness without being coerced into a doctrinaire stance.

Oates, Joyce Carol. "Honey and Bill and Dan and Celia." *New York Times Book Review*, 22 April 1979, 7, 27. Excerpts reprinted in *Contemporary Literary Criticism*, vol. 18, 310. Detroit: Gale Research, 310. Oates calls *Only Children* a triumph in the comic mode.

Rogers, Katharine M. "Alison Lurie: The Uses of Adultery," *American Women Writing Fiction: Memory, Identity, Family, Space*, edited by Mickey Pearlman, 114-34 (Lexington: University of Kentucky Press, 1989). The most comprehensive – and best – essay so far on the novels. Rogers brilliantly links Lurie's fiction through *Foreign Affairs* as showing "concern with awakening her heroines to look critically at their lives." An indispensable study.

Sage, Lorna. "Adventures in the Old World." *London Times Literary Supplement,* 1 February 1985, 109. Excerpts reprinted in *Contemporary Literary Criticism,* vol. 39, 183-84. Detroit: Gale Research, 1986. Sage believes *Foreign Affairs* exhibits "extraordinary powers of collusion" with the reader. The novel "elicits a conspiratorial glow . . . it flatters the reader unmercifully."

Sale, Roger. "The Way We Live Now." *New York Review of Books,* 8 August 1974, 32-33. Excerpts reprinted in *Contemporary Literary Criticism,* vol. 4, 306. Detroit: Gale Research, 1975. Like John Aldridge, Sale believes Lurie possesses undoubted gifts but should be better than she is. Of *The War between the Tates* he writes: "A good, eminently readable, badly flawed, occasionally touching novel."

Sanborn, Sara. "On the Way We Fight Now." *New York Times Book Review,* 28 July 1974, 1-2. Excerpts reprinted in *Contemporary Literary Criticism,* vol. 4, 305. Detroit: Gale Research, 1975. Meets *The War between the Tates* on its own comic terms and finds it "a near-perfect comedy of manners and morals to put on the shelf next to *Vanity Fair.*"

Stark, John. "Alison Lurie's Career." *Hollins Critic,* February 1989, 1-7. Stark sees in Lurie's "successful" career an instance of maturation within the same fictional territory. He finds her breakthrough in "the epistemological analysis of sociology in *Imaginary Friends.*"

Stern, Carol Simpson. Entry in *Contemporary Novelists,* 4th ed., 548-49. New York: St. Martin's, 1986. Perhaps the best of the overview essays. Stern finds the usual "influence" tie-ins to Jane Austen and Henry James "misleading" and believes Lurie's work is more aptly compared with feminist novelists Marilyn French, Erica Jong, Doris Lessing, and Joyce Carol Oates.

Wickenden, Dorothy. "Love in London." *New Republic,* 8 October 1984, 34-36. Excerpts reprinted in *Contemporary Literary Criticism,* vol. 39, 180-81. Detroit: Gale Research, 1986. Wickenden, who has admired Lurie's previous efforts, finds *Foreign Affairs* "hampered by an inability to surmount its own pettiness."

Wilkie, Everett, and Josephine Helterman. *Dictionary of Literary Biography.* vol. 2, *American Novelists since World War II,* 275-77. Detroit: Gale Research, 1978. This retrospective – up to *The War between the Tates* – views Lurie as a social critic and iconoclast who "warns us that much is in need of examination and correction and that much of what shocks us should come as no surprise."

Index

The Author

Richard Hauer Costa is professor emeritus of English at Texas A&M University, where he taught from 1970 to 1990. He worked in newspaper journalism for 14 years before beginning his teaching career at Utica College of Syracuse University in 1961. He has taught literary biography, modern British fiction, Edwardian literature, and literary analysis. In 1976 and 1984 he won university awards for distinguished teaching at Texas A&M.

Professor Costa is the author of a biographical memoir, *Edmund Wilson, Our Neighbor from Talcottville* (1980), and of critical biographies of H. G. Wells (1967, 1985) and Malcolm Lowry (1972). He is also the author of the obituary monograph on Graham Greene in *Dictionary of Literary Biography Yearbook,* 1992. His most recent book is *Safe at Home: A Baseball Wife's Story* (1989), co-authored with Sharon Hargrove. He is working on a book on the late French actor Harry Baur.

The Editor

Frank Day is a professor of English at Clemson University. He is the author of *Sir William Empson: An Annotated Bibliography* and *Arthur Koestler: A Guide to Research.* He was a Fulbright Lecturer in American Literature in Romania (1980-81) and in Bangladesh (1986-87).